woody allen
A BIOGRAPHY

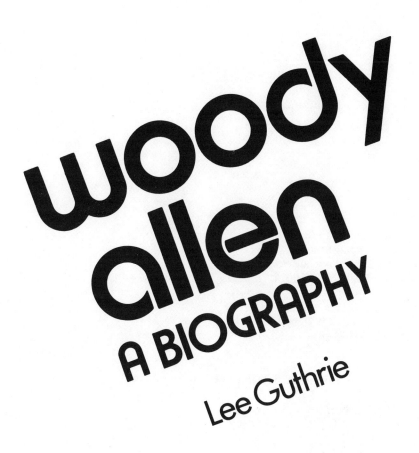

woody allen
A BIOGRAPHY

Lee Guthrie

DRAKE PUBLISHERS INC.
NEW YORK · LONDON

Published in 1978 by
Drake Publishers, Inc.
801 Second Avenue
New York, N.Y. 10017

Library of Congress Cataloging in Publication Data

Guthrie, Lee.
    Woody Allen, a biography.

        1. Allen, Woody. 2. Comedians—United States—
Biography.
PN2287.A53G8   791'.092'4 [B]   77-87469
ISBN 0-8473-1702-1

Design: Harold Franklin

Printed in the United States of America

CONTENTS

chapter 1

Beginnings

WHEN YOU THINK ABOUT BROOKLYN, Flatbush comes immediately to mind: the two are almost synonymous. The neighborhood known as Flatbush has become, according to American myth, the quintessential Brooklyn, In all those World War II propaganda movies many of us grew up on, a properly balanced cast always had to include a street-smart, wisecracking urban urchin who hailed from the vicinity of Flatbush Avenue. Completing the cast would be a good ol' boy from the South, a solid and dependable Midwesterner, a black and a Jew. Every destroyer/foxhole/flight crew, at least in the movies, could be counted on to display this positive proof that each element in the American melting pot was doing its proper share in the battle against Hitler, Mussolini, Hirohito.

So it is not entirely inappropriate that the funniest and most prolific urban urchin to appear on the American entertainment scene in the latter half of the twentieth century was spawned from the crowded streets of Flatbush. But unlike the movies' Flatbush urchins, Woody Allen did not speak in the patois of "dese", "dem", "dose" and "youse guys". Nor did he possess the blessed lack of self-awareness that the good-hearted and socially naive movie urchins could claim as part of their Brooklyn birthright.

Woody Allen, apparently from the cradle, looked on the world around him and found it totally absurd. In describing its absurdity to us, he also made us see how ridiculous, nutty and wacked-out life really is under that thin veneer known as civilization. And the looniest thing of all is our tendency to take this nuttiness seriously.

* * * * * *

Back to Woody's cradle. (*"I don't think my parents liked me. They put a live teddy bear in my crib."*) He was not yet, of course, Woody Allen. Born on December 1, 1935, under the sign of Sagittarius, he was the first son in a lower middle class Jewish household.

Nettie Cherrie of Manhattan's Lower East Side had married Martin Konigsberg of Flatbush, Brooklyn. They were now living on Avenue K in a small, shabby apartment and struggling against the Great Depression like everyone else. Proud and happy that their first child had been a boy, they named him Allen Stewart after his grandfather.

Allen Stewart Konigsberg. That would be a difficult name for a tall, well-built, outgoing extrovert to bear. But this little boy with his frayed red hair, his myopia, his quirky way of looking at the world was short, frail, underweight and very definitely introverted, even then.

"When the other kids learned my name, they beat me up. So I'd tell them my name was Frank, but they'd still beat me up."

The neighborhood was ethnically mixed. Woody has said it was "high poor". The sidewalks were tough but not murderous. *"You were cast out on the streets at seven in the morning and told not to return until midnight. You'd spend the day breaking windows, setting fires in which to explode tin cans."*

Young Allen found it hard to keep up. In later years, he especially remembered Floyd, who was adept at stealing hub caps . . . from moving cars. This hyperbole was necessary to get across the full depth of Floyd's toughness, meanness and proclivity toward being a bully.

"Floyd used to sit in the Dumb Row in school . . . a vegetable mentality in a black leather jacket. Once I was walking past the poolroom on my way to my violin lesson. Floyd yells out to me . . . 'Hey, Red!'

". . . I was a cocky kid. I put down my violin case. I walked up to him.

" 'My name is not Red. If you want me, call me by my regular name: Master . . . Heywood . . . Allen.'

(There is a long pause.)

"I spent that winter in a wheelchair . . . after a team of doctors had labored to remove a violin . . . lucky for me it wasn't a cello.

"Years later, however, Floyd and I became good friends. I removed a thorn from his paw."

Early on, Allen Stewart Konigsberg realized the value of humor as a defense. "If I got beat up when I was a kid," he remembers, "or got in trouble with the cops, I'd be scared—petrified—but I always knew I could be funny about it the next day. I could always make people laugh."

* * * * * *

Another defense was sports. Martin Konigsberg says that his son picked up the nickname "Woody" very early in life. "The kids on the block named him 'Woody' because he was always the one to bring the stick out for the stickball game. He was always athletic."

Woody Allen has described his childhood as "hectic", "miserable" and "normal". He remembers that his father had "a million little short-lived jobs." Martin Konigsberg was, among other things, a taxi-driver, a singing waiter at Sammy's Bowery Follies and a dabbler in the jewelry business.

During most of Woody's childhood, Nettie Konigsberg kept the books for a Manhattan florist shop.

Describing his family, Woody Allen has said, "They're all silly people in a grotesque way. Nerve-wrackingly silly. They're preposterous. And they can't do anything right. My father is a comical gnome who looks like Fernandel and has always been preoccupied with silly business schemes. My mother is Groucho. She is. She looks like Groucho Marx and she talks like him."

Later in life, Woody Allen solemnly declared that he was convinced his adoration of Groucho Marx contained much repressed adoration for his mother.

One reason that Woody remembers his childhood as "hectic" is that they were always moving. They were "always get-

ting billeted with relations. There were always cousins and un-
cles running in and out of rooms."

Martin Konigsberg remembers his son as being "timid
and withdrawn". Allen remembers that he "lacked for none
of the creature comforts. But I was shy, and *everything* dissatisfied me, although I don't know why. I had this intense
sense of failure. But although I never laughed out loud then, I
was a funny kid. My viewpoint was funny and I said funny
things."

In 1944, when Woody was nine years old, Nettie and
Martin Konigsberg had another child, a girl they named Letty. In spite of the difference in their ages, as soon as Letty was
old enough to know what "big brother" meant, she was
Woody's number one fan. And he loved to amuse her with
card tricks and special magic shows.

Woody's parents may have provided the bare necessities
of life, but there wasn't often money for extras, for things like
pets.

*"My parents were too poor to buy me a dog, so they got
me an ant. I called him Spot. I trained him. I was once coming home and Sheldon Finkelstein tried to bully me, and I had
Spot with me, and I said 'Kill!' and Sheldon stepped on my
ant."*

The hours Woody was forced to spend inside P.S. 99 were
not an interesting or stimulating reprieve from the life of the
streets. Quite simply, Woody Allen hated school from the
first day of his career as a schoolboy. "I never liked it. I
couldn't wait till I grew up. I was bad in spelling, worse in
grammar and I hated my teachers because everyone was a
least common denominator.

"And my teachers all loathed me," Allen says. "I never
did homework—I mean I never *ever* did homework. I'm
amazed to this day that they really expected me to go home
and work on those sleazy projects that they had outlined.

"My father and mother were called to school so often that
my friends still recognize them on the street.

"And I never ever did any extracurricular activities at
school," Woody continues. "I would go in at nine and come
back at three and would never participate in God squad or
whatever; then I'd go right into my bedroom and shut the
door—immediately. Consequently, I was able to get some

things done. I could learn an instrument. I became real adept at sleight-of-hand, which took me endless hours and which I can still do. My mother used to pass by the room and hear the coins dropping for eight hours; she just couldn't believe it."

Things didn't improve in high school. Woody describes his grades at Midwood High School, across the street from Brooklyn College, as "below average and way below average."

He scraped by in the end with a 71 average, but his 12-year sojourn in the public schools of Flatbush left him with "a very, very dim view of the American education system, from grade school on up, because the motivation is definitely not to learn anything."

Woody Allen's one-line description in one of his comedy routines of what must have been Midwood High School says it all: *"It was a school for emotionally disturbed teachers."*

But there were other compensations, other interests, other possibilities: sports, music, movies, comic books, Mickey Spillane novels and girls. Not necessarily in that order.

The young Woody Allen, desperate as only a skinny, near-sighted, small-for-his-age kid can be, used sports to be "one of the guys." Nor were sports simply a ploy for acceptance. Woody really enjoyed the pick-up street games of stickball, handball, softball.

"Most people won't believe I was quite athletic," Woody says, "but you could look it up. I had a vicious right uppercut and qualified for the Golden Gloves." The only reason he didn't participate in the tournament was that his father refused to sign the necessary permission papers. First-born Jewish sons are expected to be doctors, dentists, lawyers. Not boxers.

Woody was also the regular second baseman on the Police Athletic League's 70th Precinct team. Woody had first met the men in blue under circumstances not totally auspicious. He'd been picked up three times: for accidentally hitting a woman with his B-B gun (she was not injured), for setting a fire (outdoors) and for breaking into a school with some other boys to play ball. The police wisely decided to allow Woody to use his excess energy on one of *their* teams.

Woody remembers that he was "all-neighborhood" in everything. "I was one of those kids who played ball from seven in the morning until after dark. I was a terrific hitter in baseball, a good shot in basketball and a halfback in football."

Boxing was Woody's favorite sport; football the least favorite. (Of course, most 115 lb. boys don't even *attempt* football.) A disastrous afternoon at Brooklyn's Wingate Field may explain Woody's aversion to football.

"I was in an argument with a kid on where to put the ball," Allen says. "He pushed me and I pushed him. Then he kicked me in the groin, and while I was down he gave me a tremendous punch in the nose. It really was a great punch. It spread my nose over my face. I had to stay in the hospital a few days. Nobody believed I was just punched. They thought I was hit with a brick or something. But it was a punch. Esthetically, I had to admire it."

It was Woody's admiration for boxers Sugar Ray Robinson and Willie Pep that led to his Golden Glove ambitions.

"I think I would have been a Pep as a boxer," Woody says. "He was my size. But you never fight your idol in your dreams. He's always at ringside watching you. Nobody laid a glove on me while he was there."

Boxing was one of the first things to bring out the philosopher in Woody Allen. "A good fight has everything a playwright could ask for. You know the stories of the fighters by reading about them. You know everything about·them, which makes any sport a thousand times more enjoyable. They're in the ring alone. Nobody can help them. The fight moves toward a climax. I become totally absorbed, just as in a good play."

In baseball, Woody's loyalties were entirely reserved for the Giants. "I could roller-skate to Ebbets Field and I saw every game they played against the Dodgers for years."

The Giants' Willie Mays has always been one of the great heroes in Woody Allen's own private gallery of all-stars.

"Mays raises baseball to any art," Woody said once during the years when the great outfielder and slugger was still playing. "The way he does things is almost poetry. He *gives* something to it. I have great admiration for (Mickey) Mantle, but the impression I always got from him was that he was too strong and fast for the game. He overpowered it. This is a bad analogy, but it's like the difference in an Ingmar Bergman movie and a Fellini movie. Bergman *gives* something to it. Fellini is just technically brilliant."

The long hours that Woody spent in his room learning magic and card tricks also gave him a life-long interest. He grew up to be a far better than average poker player who still enjoys performing the occasional card trick for friends. "I get a sense of pleasure from it like a concert pianist putting his hands on the keys."

An early devotee of old-syle New Orleans Dixieland jazz, Woody Allen taught himself both the soprano saxophone and the clarinet by playing along with jazz records. Long after he had given up his daily sessions of learning card tricks, Woody continued to spend at least an hour or two every day practicing his clarinet and keeping his lip in shape.

Even so, a kid like Woody Allen had energy to burn and, like all kids, there were times when he didn't know what to do. "In the summer, when there was nothing to do, I went to the movies seven times a week. And I was glutted with comic books. I didn't read a book until I was 14 or 15. I was in my late teens before I started to read decently and discovered it was fun."

Woody Allen has made a fortune on his presumably unhappy childhood. (*"I wore my cousin's hand-me-down's— and she wasn't my size."*) But apparently there were some good times, too. In addition to the stickball games in the street, "all the kids on the block went fishing, too. We got sunfish out of Prospect Park lake and we used to spend all Saturday morning in the basement of Sears, Roebuck looking at rods we never bought. I even tied flies—I had that little vise and everything."

* * * * * *

In the Konigsberg household, according to Woody, religion was "semi-important."

"They were very old world people," he recalls. *"Their values were God and carpeting."*

Still, young Woody wore phylacteries for morning prayers like the other Orthodox kids in the neighborhood, put on his yarmulke for Temple and went to Hebrew school for eight years. Woody Allen, however, declares that he figured out there was no God when he "first learned to think" at age four or five.

But the early training had its effect. Woody Allen still feels "a sense of solemnity during Yom Kippur". He has an intimate acquaintance with "the urban Jewish mentality . . . of being racked with guilt and suffering, of feeling one step ahead of trouble and anxiety."

And how could he not have known at least something about what was happening to European Jews during the years he was growing up? The Holocaust, distant as it may have seemed to a kid in Brooklyn, surely played a role in developing that free-floating paranoia that knows something terrible can happen . . . anytime, any place.

"I was terrified of death, of being kidnapped, of being on boats and especially of the dark," Woody recalls. "I'm still not thrilled with the dark. Until a few years ago, I couldn't come home at night without checking out every single closet in the house to be sure there wasn't an enemy there out to get me."

Doing battle with his fears via humor has been a healthy process for Woody Allen's bank account. The condition of his psyche is a different matter. The Brooklyn boyhood may have been grimmer than it sounds from Woody's routines. He has been in analysis since 1959.

Allen has said that part of the reason for this is his "pathological obsession with violence . . . with getting mugged, getting beat up."

* * * * * *

"My parents sent me to interfaith camp one summer. That meant I got beat up by kids of all faiths."

"Once I was beaten up by a kid who had ten dollars worth of quarters in his fists. I go to my father who gives me two ten dollar bills to fight back, but I get beaten up again. I forget to get change."

"The other boys in my class were sockers. I was a sockee."

* * * * * *

Writer Mickey Rose was Woody Allen's best friend in high school and has collaborated with him on the scripts of *Bananas* and *Take the Money and Run*. He remembers Woody as a "terribly shy, introverted guy who hated studying and was very precocious yet unsuccessful with women, full of longings and fantasies and unusually powerful sex drives, yet hard up for girls."

Another problem that surfaced in high school was the question of his future. What would he do in life?

"All of my friends seemed to know what they wanted to do and were planning to be doctors, lawyers, analysts. They went to college and did what they said they were going to do and they've all turned out that way today."

For Woody, it wasn't so easy. He thought about being a cowboy, a magician, an athlete. *"I wanted to be an FBI man, too, but you have to be five-foot-seven and have 20-20 vision. Then I toyed with becoming a master criminal—but you have to be five-foot-seven and have 20-20 vision for that."*

Woody Allen freely admits his proficiency at schoolboy shoplifting. "I gypped things when I was younger. I was a *terrific* gyp artist. Two dozen comics! A pile of school supplies! I used to hit Woolworth's. As I got older, I thought I would be a dice and card hustler. One summer I wondered, should I go away and do magic tricks in the mountains or go into partnership with a guy and hustle crap games in Brooklyn."

Woody decided the hustle in Brooklyn was his best course of action. The project turned out well: "We would make $10 or $20 a night."

There was never, of course, the merest thought of violent crime. Woody Allen was never into mugging, armed robbery or homicide. "Basically, my propensities are intellectual. Gambling, hustling, confidence swindling—the esthetics appealed to me."

Something else that has always appealed to Woody Allen is the esthetics of putting on interviewers. He has mastered the art of giving an outrageous and totally specious reply to a writer's questions with an earnest and deadpan aura of perfect seriousness.

Still, most of these put-ons are enormously funny and, in their own way, tell the careful observer just as much—or more—about Woody as a straight and honest answer.

Here's the kernel of seriousness in Woody Allen's fantasies about being a con artist: "To consign one's life to a meaningless round of subway rides, to do that hot and cold for 40 years, is not being alive at all. There's no comparison between that and a life of crime."

All along, Woody had been making up jokes, most often aimed at himself, for the benefit of schoolmates and family. It had never occurred to him that something that was so easy for him to do could also be a way of making money.

"We had a vague relative who was a press agent at the time, and when I used to make up these one-line gags, he would ask, 'Why don't you send them in to the newspaper columnists, Winchell and the rest?' So I did."

So I did. Could anything have been easier than the formal beginning of Woody Allen's career as a humorist?

The first joke survives, thanks to columnist Earl Wilson who retrieved it from an early 1950's column:

"Woody Allen says he ate at a restaurant that had O.P.S. prices—over people's salaries."

Woody placed one-liners like that by the dozen. "It was a way to get your name in the paper, and kind of fun."

Years later, when the skinny Brooklyn schoolboy had achieved fame, wealth and success, Earl Wilson looked through his columns for January, 1953, and discovered three Woody Allen jokes. Nearly twenty years later, in August, 1972, he reprinted them for his readers:

"Taffy Tuttle (Earl Wilson's fictitious showgirl) told Woody Allen she heard of a man who was a six-footer, and he said, 'Gee, it must take him a long time to put his shoes on.' "

"It's the fallen women who are usually picked up," says Woody Allen.

"Woody Allen boasts that he just made a fortune downtown—he auctioned off his parking space."

* * * * * *

Eventually, these gems were noticed by press agent David O. Alber who needed a gag-writer to put funny lines in the mouths of people like Arthur Murray, Guy Lombardo and Sammy Kaye.

Alber finally tracked Woody down through Earl Wilson

and could hardly believe the boffo lines he'd been seeing in all the papers had emerged from the head of an anemic-looking Brooklyn high school boy.

"*You're* the one? My God!"

But what the hell, a joke was a joke. Alber promptly hired schoolboy Allen to come in after school and write fifty gags a week for Alber's show-biz clients.

"Every day after school," Woody remembers, "I would take the subway to Manhattan. I gave them fifty jokes a day. They kept saying they didn't need that many but it was easy— I wrote most of them on the subway from Brooklyn and then sat around their office reading the paper until 6 o'clock. They used to give me talks about the way I dressed. I came over in my school clothes."

And make no mistake about it. Woody Allen, reluctant student at Midwood High School, loved that after-school job. "I was utterly thrilled," Woody says. "I thought I was in the heart of show business."

Then things began to happen very quickly. Allen was contacted by the William Morris Agency. Could they represent the boy gagster?

Why not? So Woody Allen, still in high school, began writing comedy sketches for Peter Lind Hayes, Pat Boone, Herb Shriner, Buddy Hackett.

"I kept getting more money all the time until finally I was making over a hundred dollars a week while I was still in my teens. I suddenly started reading then—everything I could, fiction, nonfiction, poetry, plays."

Even after the long-awaited graduation from Midwood High School, it never occurred to Woody Allen to become a full-time comedy writer. His parents expected him to go to college and learn how to do something serious, something with a secure future.

Dutifully, he enrolled at New York University. After all, it was bound to be better than Midwood High School, right? Wrong . . . it was worse. "I only went to college because my parents couldn't imagine it otherwise."

Every day, Woody got on the subway in Brooklyn and headed for NYU's Greenwich Village campus. Almost every day he didn't get off at Eighth Street where he was supposed to, but just continued on uptown.

"I did not like elementary school, or high school, and I liked college the least of the three," Woody recalls. "I was working and I was impatient to be working even more. When the subway got near Washington Square, there would always be this dilemma. 'Do I get off today and go to school?' Usually I just closed my eyes and shot by. It was such a *pleasure* not to show up.

"I had enrolled at NYU as a motion picture major. I didn't know anything about it at all and had no interest in it except that I had been movie-crazy as a kid. I went to the movies every day—a double bill, seven days a week. On Saturdays, in the old Flatbush Theater in Brooklyn, where I grew up, you could see two movies, five cartoons and a group of vaudeville acts besides. It was wonderful. I'm crazy about the old Marx Brothers comedies, *Monkey Business*, *Duck Soup*, *Horsefeathers* and the rest, and W.C. Fields."

But Woody Allen's passion for the classics of 1930's Hollywood comedy didn't do him much good at NYU. "I never actually failed a college course," Woody declares. "It was always a very indefinite 'D'. It meant you seemed to know what you were talking about, but they didn't really want to pass you."

Woody Allen lasted less than three months at NYU. He says that when he told his mother what had happened, she quietly went into the bathroom and took an overdose of mahjongg tiles.

Ever the dutiful son, Woody enrolled in night school at the City College of New York. His demise there was even swifter than it had been at NYU.

He was asked to leave both schools, he says, because of "an involvement in a number of catastrophic occurrences."

"Most of these had to do with my rebellion against censorship," Woody says. "The faculty always felt that what I wrote was not suitable material for use in the schools. They expected me to take things seriously."

Martin and Nettie Konigsberg were not happy about their son's *persona non grata* status in Manhattan's halls of academe. Ten years after Woody Allen's brush with higher education he said that "even now my parents would feel much better if I had lived up to their dream and been a pharmacist.

There's tremendous pressure where I come from—a middle-class Jewish neighborhood—to be an optometrist or a dentist or a lawyer, and that's what my friends have become. They exhibited at an early age an ability to get along at summer camp."

It was as if getting booted out of college enabled Woody Allen to finally become a grown-up . . . or his own version of a grown-up. The year he was nineteen, Woody Allen became a full-time staff writer for NBC, acquired his first Manhattan apartment, got married and went into analysis.

His school days were over and it couldn't have happened to more deserving non-student.

"To this day," Woody said years later, "I wake up in the morning and clutch onto my bed and thank God I don't have to go to school."

Soon he was making $1500 weekly for turning out sketches for, among others, Sid Caesar. Woody Allen was one of the inmates in the writers' loony bin that Caesar maintained. Other inmates, at various times, had included Carl Reiner, Mike Nichols and Elaine May, and Mel Brooks whom legend had it would dive off the filing cabinets and chew on table legs when the going got rough.

"It was totally insane," Woody says. "You sat around flinging lines at each other—pastrami sandwiches on a tough day—and the process got to be almost unconscious. This thing would come out of your mouth, completely absurd, and a minute later you'd realize, my God, that's really funny."

Woody Allen spent several years honing his comedic gifts in the writers' stables of other comics. And it was also during this period that Woody left the William Morris Agency and got himself represented by Jack Rollins and Charles Joffe, two big-time theatrical agents.

Almost immediately, Rollins and Joffe, in the best wheeler-dealer tradition, began to tell young Woody that he ought to perform his own stuff instead of putting his best lines into somebody's else's mouth.

Woody Allen's first reaction was that they were crazy. "The emotional terror of getting up in front of people has always been gigantic," Woody maintains.

He felt that he was primarily a writer and since he was doing well as a writer, why try something in which he might fall flat on his face?

As a 21-year-old writer, he had won a Sylvania award for penning a Sid Caesar special that was voted the "best comedy show of the year." Why tamper with success?

By this time, Woody was working on *The Garry Moore Show*. In many ways, he was still very much the Flatbush babe-in-the-woods wandering loose in the big city. The story is told that he was once discovered standing in line to get tickets for Garry Moore's show—he was the show's writer—because he felt shy about asking the producer for the tickets he needed.

* * * * * *

During his brief stint as a college student, Woody Allen had met Harlene Rosen, a 16-year-old freshman at Hunter College. Mickey Rose, Woody's pal from Midwood High School, says Harlene was introverted, sensitive and artistic, traits that could also be used to describe Woody. They were married shortly after Woody and CCNY parted company and it should have been a marriage made in heaven but it wasn't.

The marriage was stormy, tumultuous, unhappy. In five years, it was over. And, as usual, Woody translated his pain, anger and bitterness into humor, all of it at his ex-wife's expense.

* * * * * *

"It was partially my fault we got divorced. I had a tendency to place my wife under a pedestal."

"They called and told me my wife was violated on the streets of New York, and I said, 'If I know my wife, it wasn't a moving violation.'"

"We were always having these long philosophical discussions. She was too smart for me. She could always prove I didn't exist."

"I saw my ex-wife the other day. She was looking very

well. Of course, I hardly recognized her with her wrists closed."

* * * * * *

After several years of hearing jokes like this on national television, Harlene filed a one million dollar lawsuit against Woody, charging defamation of character. Possibly because of Harlene's lawsuit, Woody's remarks about his ex-wife became considerably more tempered, at least to interviewers.

"What happened to the marriage? I don't know but I guess we were both too young. I was 19 and she was even younger and it wasn't good for either of us."

Woody obviously made an effort to emphasize the positive aspects of the experience. "I'm glad I was married. In that time, I put my wife through college. It really blossomed her. And I count it as an extremely valuable experience for me. It introduced me to a million things I probably wouldn't have known about."

At about the time he was married, Woody began psychoanalysis. "I was very unhappy," he says. "No particular reason, just a feeling I couldn't shake, but it was a terrible, terrifying feeling to have. There was a continual awareness of seemingly unmotivated depression."

In an oblique reference to his numerous on-stage zingers aimed at Harlene, Woody said, "Despite what you might think, there is no animosity between us. We both gained a lot by being married. We were very young, though, and grew fast in other directions."

Of course, his parents took it very hard, especially Woody's mother.

"She took it rather badly, I thought. She put down her knitting, walked over to the furnace and got in."

Woody also made public the details of the divorce settlement.

"My wife got the house, the car, the bank account and if I marry again and have children, she gets them, too."

Through all of this, Harlene said nothing for public consumption. Living on West Eleventh Street in Greenwich Village, Harlene even had her phone disconnected in order to stop phone calls from reporters and columnists.

* * * * * *

It took a couple of years of badgering before Jack Rollins and Charles Joffe were able to persuade Woody that he'd be better off performing his own material instead of frustrating his creativity by putting it into the television shows and night club routines of other comics.

As Woody Allen tells it, Jack Rollins' campaign to turn Woody into a performer took the form of cracks on the head, relentless pestering and middle-of-the-night phone calls.

Rollins and Joffe were hardly philanthropists. ("Son, we're doing this for your own good!") The simple, bottom-line fact is that ten per cent of a performer usually adds up to considerably more than ten per cent of a writer.

The factor that tipped the balance in favor of Rollins and Joffe was Woody's fervent admiration for Mort Sahl, a complex, possibly self-destructive but clearly brilliant and innovative comedian, who was busy restructuring the art of comedy in the late Fifties and early Sixties.

"He (Sahl) changed the face of comedy the way Stravinsky changed music," Woody says.

It was a change that Woody Allen decided he wanted to be part of, so when Rollins and Joffe booked him into a tiny Village bistro called Upstairs at the Duplex, what could he say but . . . yes, he'd do it.

The only problem was that he was working all day as a writer for Garry Moore and he could hardly afford to quit since the gig at the Duplex didn't pay anything.

Except, of course, experience, exposure, and a chance to develop expertise.

chapter 2

Nightclubs

and Television

ONE OF THE MOST SHATTERING DECADES in American history—the 1960's—began, strangely enough, with immense creative energy, style and idealistic vision. In his Inauguration Address, the youthful and narrowly elected President John F. Kennedy promised the torch had been passed to a new generation that would "ask not what your country can do for you but what you can do for your country."

As it happens, the 1960's saw more asking of the federal government for grants, fellowships, farm price supports, housing subsidies, food stamps, defense contract over-runs and other hand-outs than ever before in U.S. history. This and other darker aspects of the decade such as the Vietnam war had not yet, however, begun to emerge.

There was a new political style in Washington, at least on the surface, and the possibility of Camelot on the Potomac seemed neither absurd nor far-fetched. As an almost organic manifestation of the winds of change, a whole new generation of comics had suddenly breezed in out of nowhere.

Mort Sahl led the pack. And Sahl, with his biting, caustic and uncomfortably relevant social and political satire, had no more ardent disciple than a young television comedy writer named Woody Allen, who thought of Mort Sahl as "an original genius who revolutionized the medium."

"Sahl's whole approach was different," Woody has said. "It wasn't that he did political comment—as everyone keeps insisting. It was that he had genuine insights. Without him, we wouldn't have had *Beyond the Fringe* or Bob Newhart. He made the country receptive to a kind of comedy it wasn't used to hearing.

"I'd always admired standup comics," Woody continued. Guys like (Jack) Benny, (Milton) Berle, Henny Youngman, (Bob) Hope. They were tremendous talents, well developed. I still believe that being a standup comic is the best education you can get. Mine came largely from watching Mort Sahl. He made the country listen to jokes that required them to think. Watching him made me want to be a standup comedian.

"He was like Charlie Parker in jazz. There was a need for a revolution, everybody was ready for a revolution, but some guy had to come along who could perform the revolution and be great. Mort was the one. He was like the tip of the iceberg. Underneath were all the other people who came along: Lenny Bruce, Nichols and May, all the Second City players. I'm not saying that these people wouldn't have happened anyway, but Mort was the vanguard of the group that had an enormous renaissance of nightclub comedy that ended not long after Bill Cosby and I came along. He totally restructured comedy. His jokes are laid down with such guile. He changed the rhythm of jokes. He had different content, surely, but the revolution was in the way he laid the jokes down."

It took a long time, however, for Woody to make the transition from writer to performer, in spite of his admiration for Sahl whom he first saw in 1953. Woody had known from early childhood that he could make people laugh. "But doing it in public is hard. Some people are extroverts and they grow up to be the performers. Some people are introverts and they're the writers. Did you know that George S. Kaufman was shy . . . sensationally introverted? I'm an introvert. I was a writer first. It took me a long time to be a professional comic."

Apparently, for a number of years, Woody Allen was torn between following in the footsteps of Mort Sahl or imitating a literary idol from his youth. "I fell in love with the playwright George S. Kaufman when I was very young. I don't know why. I watched him when he was on television in a panel show and something about him just took me over. I patterned myself after him in every way I could. I tried to look like him; I cultivated a sardonic manner; I was aloof and didn't communicate with people. I was extremely shy and reserved in my behavior.

"When I saw Jason Robards play Kaufman in *Act One*, the first time the movie cut to Kaufman, in the scene where he was on the telephone, my heart gave a big thump. I even remember when I was in the third grade in grammar school —I couldn't have been more than nine years old, maybe not that much—and we were sent to the library to learn how to look up books. I happened to pick up a copy of plays by Kaufman and Hart and I began reading *You Can't Take It with You* and read, 'The scene is . . . just around the corner from Columbia University but don't go looking for it,' and I thought to myself that was funny."

* * * * * *

And then it couldn't be put off any longer. The unpaid gig that Rollins and Joffe had arranged for him at the Duplex began. After his daily tour of duty on the Garry Moore show was over, Woody would go home, try to get a few hours' rest and then head downtown to the Village.

"It was winter. I'd stand out in the cold at night, shivering and trying to get a cab to go downtown and wondering why I was doing it."

It would be nice to report that Woody Allen was an instant, smash success, but he wasn't. He was, in fact, perfectly terrible. The early audiences were concerned: they thought he looked ill. Little did they know that if he had actually been as ill as he looked, he'd have been in the hospital. Naturally, his fears affected his performance . . . or lack thereof.

Manager Rollins was there and remembers it well. "He was so tense and nervous that he kept fiddling with the cord until we thought he would choke himself. He would just read his lines with no art of delivery and the audience would wonder what kind of wild animal is this.

"He was a bomb, but Woody's got the guts of a second story man and he continued to go out there every night. Then one day he asked Charlie and me if we thought maybe he shouldn't forget about being a standup comic and go back to writing where he was very successful."

Manager Joffe says that Woody was "just awful. Of course he had good lines. But he was so scared and embarrassed and—rabbity. Either John or I watched both his shows every night. We were afraid he might run off and never come back if we weren't there to watch him."

Charles Joffe took his responsibilities as Woody's agent very seriously: Joffe didn't miss Woody's act even on his wedding day. he and his new bride showed up—she was still in her wedding dress—and sat through both shows.

Woody Allen, professional and congenital introvert, still shudders when he is forced to recall leaving "a nice, safe, warm typewriter and go out into the freezing cold to stand on a bare stage and make a fool of myself.

"It was unspeakably agonizing," he continues. "I didn't know what I was doing. All day long, I would shake and tremble, thinking about standing up that night before people and trying to be funny.

"There were never very many people in the club, maybe a dozen or more, and I went on night after night trying to win them over.

"I worked at the Duplex for a year," Woody says. "It was the worst year of my life. I'd feel this fear in my stomach the minute I woke up, and it would be there until I went on at 11 o'clock at night. I'd have a sensation of relief after I finished the second show but the next morning it would start all over again. I was fired from *The Garry Moore Show*. I didn't blame them. I hated that job. It was too much like school. You were supposed to show up every morning and I didn't. But after that I wasn't making a cent. I was breaking up with my first wife . . ."

* * * * * *

"My wife was extremely childish. One time I was taking a bath and she just walked right in and sank all by boats."

"The Museum of Natural History took her shoe, and based on the measurement, they reconstructed a dinosaur."

"My wife and I pondered whether to take a vacation or get a divorce, and we decided that a trip to Bermuda is over in two weeks, but a divorce is something you always have."

* * * * * *

"I'd started out thinking I could be funny if my material was funny. But I began finding out that you have to be a performer. A big comedian—Bob Hope—could be funny if he had to go on without any lines at all. Also I was trying to be cerebral. I was writing for dogs with high-pitched ears, but the people couldn't hear me. I didn't think I'd ever be able to change. It was so embarrassing getting up there every night. Sometimes there would only be two or three people at the second show and if I remembered seeing one of them at the first show it just killed me—repeating myself like that."

Woody confessed years later to an ulterior motive behind his persistence.

"By then I knew that I wanted to be a playwright, but I realized that would take several years of concentrated work. Until that time came along, I felt that working on a night club act would help me understand what it was to be a performer, like an actor with an audience, and it would also function in terms of creating material—the way you might write poetry while you were working on a novel."

Still, trying to be both writer and performer was a feat Woody found extremely difficult. "When you're a writer," he observed, "you're alone most of the time. Your eccentricities become charming, theatrical. Writers tend to be terribly theatrical—they claim not to be, but they are, with their beards, turtlenecks. It's a radical departure to go for eight or ten years as a writer and then become a performer. You're the opposite of alone. Your private life is laid so open to the public that the tendency is to behave slightly more normal or people will think you're an oddball. Everything you do, you do knowing you're doing it publicly and not anonymously.

"I'd avoided it (performing) for a long time. When I was sixteen and decided to be a writer—and I eventually wanted to write *serious* things, like for *The New Yorker*—it was in part because I was terrified of dealing with people, and I wanted to remain isolated. So it was an enormous wrench for me to go from the most ideally isolated situation to the most public situation available. It happens overnight," Woody recalls. "You decide you're going to do it and you're trapped, and the number of people doesn't make a difference. You're as terrified of performing for twenty people in a club at 3:00 a.m. as you are for 20,000 people in an auditorium.

"I found I could be distracted by lots of things. One night I watched a prizefight on TV before I went on and after being such a nervous wreck watching the fight I didn't feel like doing a thing. I'm crazy about fights. I don't know why exactly except that I'm small and it means a lot to me somehow. I'm what I would consider a peaceful person and I never fight with anyone."

In spite of the terrors of performing, however, Woody Allen quickly learned the basics of the art of standup comedy. "The simple fundamentals of working in clubs can be unequivocally learned in a month. This business about needing '10 years of experience' has no meaning to me. I learned all about the controllable externals in a couple of weeks, and I think these instincts are either inborn, or else give up—it's hopeless."

* * * * * *

Slowly, Woody Allen constructed the Woody Allen persona. It was a process that didn't happen overnight. He used his own natural shyness as a conscious tool. He noticed which lines got the most laughs, and when he discovered that the most effective gags had to do with his own sense of ineptness he began expanding those themes in his routines.

* * * * * *

"I have slow reflexes. I was once run over by a car with a flat tire that was being pushed by two guys."

"I wear suit size 32 dwarf. When I buy suits, they always send me to the boys' department. It's inhuman when six-year-olds try on suits next to you."

"When we played softball, I'd steal second, then feel guilty and go back."

"As a boy I was ashamed to wear glasses. I went to an optometrist, he called out the letters and I'd answer true or false."

* * * * * *

Gradually, he was becoming a real comedian with his own unique comic self in the same way that Jack Benny, Bob Hope, Milton Berle and Groucho Marx were unique. These men were effective because of the personality each projected, not because the lines they actually delivered were intrinsically funnier than the guy who is hopelessly stalled in the Vegas lounges, trying to get laughs with the bathroom jokes that everybody first heard in fourth grade.

"Suppose I draw a rabbit on a piece of paper," Woody says, by way of illustrating his thesis that it's all but impossible to pin down the essence of a comedian's success. "Then Picasso comes along and he draws a rabbit. By *nature* Picasso's rabbit just has to be interesting. Just his pencil line has got *feeling*, though he may not do anything fancy. It's like that with comedians, too.

"To this day, if you hear (the late) Groucho (Marx) talk, there's something in his voice, like there is in Picasso's line. It's not *what* he's saying. It's his style. There's no way to explain it. All the best comedians, Chaplin, the Marx Brothers, Hope, Benny, Berle. These guys are great talents. It's a gift and they were born with it."

As Woody refined his act at the Duplex during that long and lonely year, it gradually caught on. The little room was full every night. Then, during the fall of 1962, he was invited uptown for a two-week engagement at the Blue Angel, a trendy supper club that took pride in showcasing bright, new performers early in their careers.

To his amazement, the critics were almost unanimous in their enthusiasm. He went back downtown, but this time to The Bitter End, a Greenwich Village coffeehouse that flourished during the folk-singing revival of the early Sixties.

At this point, the *New York Times* took notice.

Entertainment writer Arthur Gelb said, "The most refreshing comic to emerge in many months is a slight, bespectacled, unhappy-looking, former sketch writer of 26 named Woody Allen.

"He has hunched shoulders, an air of harassment, a carefully cultivated nebbish quality and a line of patter that, for a wonder, eschews any references to the President and his family.

"Mr. Allen approaches the microphone on the unadorned platform at The Bitter End . . . as though he were afraid it would bite him.

"As it turns out, he *is* afraid it will bite him. For grotesque hazards stalk Mr. Allen 24 hours a day. He is a Chaplinesque victim with an S.J. Perelman sense of the bizarre and a Mort Sahl delivery (despite the fact that he steers clear of topical material).

"Mr. Allen will be at The Bitter End five weeks for anyone who is interested in watching a rising young comic develop into an established young comic.

"The impertinent, the irreverent and ludicrous flow from him in an almost endless stream."

Clearly, Woody was on his way to bigger and better things, and with the imprimatur of favorable newspaper reviews, network television executives were willing to take a chance that Allen's quirky humor wouldn't offend the average viewer out there in Middle America. And they were relieved that Allen didn't use the kind of political satire indulged in by the likes of Mort Sahl and Lenny Bruce. The men who ran television wanted ratings, not controversy which they found to be only slightly less distasteful than bubonic plague.

During 1963, Woody Allen broke out of his Manhattan cocoon and became a national personality. He appeared on most of the major variety shows: Ed Sullivan, Merv Griffin, *The Tonight Show, Hootenanny* and *Candid Camera*.

He played the college circuit as well as clubs like Mister Kelly's in Chicago, the hungry i in San Francisco. And a one-night stand to a packed house in Carnegie Hall.

The New York papers kept track of his schedule. Major

stories and profiles began to appear. Time Magazine devoted one and one-half columns to rising young comic Woody Allen whom they described as "his own Boswell."

* * * * * *

"There was a time I wanted to be a spy, but spies have to swallow microfilm, and my doctor says I can't have celluloid."

"I was classified 4P by my draft board. In the event of war, I'm a hostage."

"I tried to rub one stick together to make a fire. This is very Zen—not Boy Scout."

"I carry a sword for protection. In case of attack, I press the handle and the sword turns into a cane—and I beg for sympathy."

* * * * * *

"Since I began performing, I find my whole personality has been changing a great deal. From being like George S. Kaufman, I've had to become warm and friendly and relate to the people who listen to me. If an audience doesn't like you, you're finished. After I'm through at a club, or especially if I've been on television the night before, if I can help it, I won't go out of the house for a day or two. I feel terribly ashamed—maybe shy is a better word—but I can't bear the idea of people looking at me and recognizing me and saying to themselves, 'That's Woody Allen.' I sign autographs, of course, and I'm polite to people, but I can't really bear it. I go to great lengths to avoid coming into contact with people after leaving TV studios, like taking the elevator down to the basement and leaving by another entrance, even disguising myself if I can.

"I draw my material from things that happen to me, like my parents, my school, marriage. Some of it's true, some of it isn't. I don't care which as long as it gets a laugh. For example, I've got to go to the bank today because they won't cash one of my checks—I don't know why—and straighten things out. Three weeks from now, that will suddenly turn up as a new piece of material. Nights when I feel bored, I experiment with new routines, to see how they go over. I love performing. It's funny, now when I come on, people start laughing at the clothes I'm wearing, at the very sight of me, before I do anything at all. Maybe a whole minute goes by before it's quiet enough for me to start talking. I work on funny lines but what I'm really interested in is creating an image of a warm person that people will accept as funny, apart from the joke or the gag."

By this time, Woody was living in a three-room apartment at 74th and Park Avenue. After the break-up of his marriage to Harlene, he'd been living in a one-room apartment, *"subdivided by the landlord into living quarters,"* which had been robbed so often *"I finally hung a sign on the door: We gave."*

"I like being completely casual and informal at work—although I wish they wouldn't serve drinks while I'm on the stage. I noticed at one club I played that no one would be seated at the front tables unless he slipped the headwaiter a five-dollar bill. Sometimes the whole club would be filled except the tables right in front of me and then in the middle of the act a group of four of five people would shuffle down front . . .

"But I like playing nightclubs—it keeps me close to people. I enjoy going out to clubs in different cities, too. You can get a lot of work done that way. I don't know anyone in those places, so I have all day to work."

* * * * * *

"I went to N.Y.U. I got into the philosophy department, and I took all the abstract philosophy courses, like Truth and Beauty, Advanced Truth and Beauty, Introduction to God, Death 101 . . . I was thrown out of college for cheating on my metaphysics final. I looked within the soul of the boy sitting next to me."

"I'm afraid many members of my family are eccentric. You see this watch? This is an absolutely fantastic, very fine, elegant gold watch, which speaks of breeding, and was sold to me by my grandfather . . . on his deathbed."

"My grandfather had a wonderful funeral. It was a catered funeral with accordion players and a buffet table, and there was a replica of the deceased in potato salad."

* * * * * *

My material varies from show to show; I check with the headwaiter to see if anyone has stayed over from the first show and if someone has, I change my act. Sometimes I can make awful mistakes with my stuff. I may go into stories about being divorced in front of a college crowd, or tell how I was kicked out of school to a middle-aged group and they won't find it funny. Then other times the college people will find stories of my divorce very funny and laugh their heads off. You can never tell.

"One night I heard someone whisper my punch line just before I came to it. I stopped immediately and switched to another story, but I don't think most people noticed. I draw from twelve or fifteen different routines and usually go on for thirty-five minutes, but if I know the people out there are really watching me, I'll stay on longer. There doesn't seem to be any respectable limit to how long you can use the same piece of material. People like to hear things over and over again . . ."

* * * * * *

"I shot a moose once. I was hunting in upstate New Yo and I shot a moose and I strap him onto the fender of my and I'm driving home. But what I didn't realize was that bullet hadn't penetrated the moose, it had just creased scalp, knocking him unconscious. And I'm driving thro the Holland Tunnel and the moose woke up. So I'm driy with a live moose on my fender. The moose is signalling j turn and there's a law in New York State against driving a conscious moose on your fender on Tuesdays, Thurs and Saturdays. And I'm very panicky and then it hits some friends of mine are having a costume party. I'll g take the moose. I'll ditch him at the party. Then it wo my responsibility. So I drive up to the party, I knock c

door, the moose is next to me. My host comes to the door. I say, 'Hello . . . you know the Solomons.' We enter. The moose mingles. Did very well. Scored. Some guy was trying to sell him insurance for an hour and a half. Twelve o' clock comes. They give out prizes for the best costume of the night . . . First prize goes to the Berkowitzes, a married couple dressed as a moose. The moose comes in second. The moose is furious. He and the Berkowitzes lock antlers in the living room. They knock each other unconscious. Now I figure, here's my chance. I grab the moose, strap him to my fender and shoot back to the woods . . . but . . . I got the Berkowitzes. So I'm driving along with two Jewish people on my fender which is against the law in New York State . . . Tuesdays, Thursdays . . . and especially Saturdays. The following morning the Berkowitzes wake up in the woods in a moose suit. Mr. Berkowitz is shot, stuffed and mounted . . . at the New York Athletic Club.

"But the joke is on them . . . cause it's restricted."

* * * * * *

"I don't know why people find me funny, why they laugh at me. I can't tell you what I *am*, but I can tell you what I'm *not*. I'm not 'fey' and I'm not 'Chaplinesque' and, above all, I'm not 'cerebral'. Why does a pair of glasses automatically make you cerebral? Sex and death are two fairly elementary subjects, and they are my two biggest themes—because they interest me the most, I guess.

"I suppose my humor appeals to people because I look at things differently. My reactions to everyday situations seem normal to me, but completely hilarious to everyone else, and most of the time I can't figure out why."

At about the time he began his apprenticeship at the Duplex, Woody met Louise Lasser, a perky young woman who had dropped out of Brandeis University in order to come to New York and become an actress and singer. The two hit it off instantly. Louise's company did much to alleviate the trauma of those nearly two years after Woody's first marriage had broken up and he had left the security and anonymity of

his successful writer's life for the doubts and painful exposure involved in being a fledgling performer.

Woody Allen has described Louise Lasser as a "high-style, utterly urban, intensely neurotic comedienne. You can spot her neurosis immediately in her voice, in her phrasing, in her fingertips." Woody felt that two such well-matched neurotics as he and Louise should work together, but Louise resisted.

"I'm not a comedienne," the future Mary Hartman said. "I don't know what makes you think I'm funny."

Another friend from those years is Dick Cavett who was then working for Jack Paar as a writer. Paar sent Cavett to The Duplex to catch Woody's act. Word was getting around that a bright, new talent was emerging downtown. Cavett was smitten by Woody's approach to humor. "The minute I walked in that night," he says, "the sound of the material was so high; I couldn't believe that he could go on so well for twenty minutes with this level of wonderful stuff."

* * * * * *

"I was kidnapped once. I was standing in front of my schoolyard and a black sedan pulls up and these two guys get out and they say to me, do I want to go away with them to a land where everybody is fairies and elves and I can have all the comic books I want, and chocolate buttons and wax lips. And I said, yes. And I got into the car with them, 'cause I figured, what the hell, I was home anyhow that weekend from college.

"They drive me off and they send a ransom note to my parents. My father has bad reading habits so he gets into bed at night with the ransom note and he reads half of it. Then he got drowsy and fell asleep.

"Meanwhile, they take me to New Jersey, bound and gagged. My parents finally realize that I'm kidnapped. They snap into action immediately: they rent out my room. The ransom note says for my father to leave $1000 in a hollow tree in New Jersey. He has no trouble raising the $1000 but he gets a hernia carrying the hollow tree.

"The FBI surround the house. 'Throw the kid out,' they say. 'Give us your guns and come out with your hands up.'

"The kidnappers say, 'We'll throw the kid out. Let us keep our guns and get to our car.'

"The FBI says, 'Throw the kid out. We'll let you get to your car. Give us your guns.'

"The kidnappers say, 'We'll throw the kid out. Let us keep our guns. We don't have to get to our car.'

"The FBI says, 'Keep the kid.'

"The FBI decides to lob in tear gas . . . but they don't have tear gas. Several of the agents put on the death scene from Camille. *Tear-stricken, my abductors give themselves up. They're sentenced to 15 years on a chain-gang. But they escape—twelve of them—chained together at the ankle, getting by the guards posing as an immense charm bracelet."*

* * * * * *

Late in 1963, after over a year of incredible successes, Woody Allen believed that his education as a performer had hardly begun. He confesses that he still did not know how to handle an unresponsive audience.

"There are performers who, under those circumstances, will go out and really put on a crash program. I'm just learning how to do that and it's thrilling," Woody declared.

It was a skill that didn't come easily. Occasionally, Woody found an audience so obtuse that he didn't think they were worth further effort on his part. Dick Cavett remembers one night when Woody was playing a club date in L.A.: "About twelve gems in a row had gone by unrecognized by the audience who sat there stupidly blinking at the lights. He just came to a complete stop. There was an awful long moment where nobody knew if he was going to go on or what."

Finally, Woody spoke. "If I were giving prizes for the worst audience I've ever seen, you'd win it."

Nobody laughed at that either . . . but then, they weren't supposed to. Woody freely admitted that he responded much better to love than to indifference. "As soon as I find out I'm accepted," he said, "there's no controlling me."

In his very early interviews, Woody Allen comes across as relatively candid and sincere. He had not yet, perhaps, realized that the artificial comic persona he had created for his nightclub act would be taken as a one-on-one match with his real self.

"I never used to think I was a persecuted Wally Cox figure until people began telling me so," he said. "And I even sort of resented it. I felt I was telling my personal problems to people and I resented that my problems came across as persecution. I've suddenly realized that people expect a comedian to be funny when he's being interviewed, even when he's not 'performing' and ordinarily I'm not. Now I'm writing things for me to say in interviews. Since I've become better known, though, writers come and watch me perform and then write articles which present me as something not quite the way I am, like a person overwhelmed by his environment and that sort of thing, building an image I don't see at all.

"I don't see myself as a loser. When I started performing, I thought of myself as exactly the opposite. I've always offered myself as a lover, a sportsman, a raconteur, a defender of the faith—all the good things—and not in any way a bumbler. But the audience would always laugh."

If that, however, was the way the game was played, he'd be happy to go along. It took only a slight shift of emphasis, a few embellished details. A hard-edged and easily understood public image, even if erroneous, was apparently a necessary part of an entertainer's basic equipment. Soon Woody was saying things to reporters that underlined the performer's self rather than his own private self which was obviously not at all like the bumbling, incompetent little nebbish so beloved of his audiences.

So Woody Allen started saying things like this: "I like to brood a lot and I like to sit unhappily by myself listening to music and reading."

To another reporter, he said: "Laugh if you like, but I consider myself attractive, virile, literate, a scholar, an acid wit—all in all, a sort of intellectual Cary Grant.

"You're like all the rest. You laugh because I'm really five and a half feet tall, weigh 125 pounds, wear thick glasses and have odd-looking red hair."

* * * * * *

"A girlfriend introduced me to a pseudo-post-impressionist artist who unsuccessfully tried to cut off his ear with an electric razor."

"I do not believe in an afterlife although I am bringing a change of underwear."

"A huge dog began chasing me. It was the kind of dog that chases automobiles—and brings them back."

"I took a course in rapid reading. For the final I read War and Peace *in twenty minutes. It deals with Russia."*

* * * * * *

One night in 1964 a middle-aged movie producer named Charles K. Feldman caught the last show at the Blue Angel with his friend, Shirley MacLaine. Feldman nursed a couple of drinks and listened intently to the little red-headed comic at the mike. Feldman had never heard such zany humor since Perelman was writing for the Marx Brothers back in the Thirties.

Suddenly, Charlie Feldman had an inspiration. It came out of left field which was fine with him: some of his very best inspirations had come, unannounced, out of left field.

Charlie Feldman's inspiration came in the form of a question. Would the little red-headed comic like to take a crack at rewriting the script for a movie that Feldman was trying to get off the ground?

chapter 3

Hollywood

and Broadway:

Expanded Ambitions

CHARLIE FELDMAN STARTED his working life as a lawyer. Then he got bored writing the contracts for other people's deals, so he became an agent. He represented some of Hollywood's biggest names: Greta Garbo, Marilyn Monroe, Marlene Dietrich, Gary Cooper, John Wayne, Richard Burton.

According to Feldman, he was the agent who made the first deal in which the star got a percentage of the box-office take. He performed this financial miracle first for John Wayne; others followed.

Eventually, however, representing other people proved not totally satisfactory and Feldman turned producer. Here, too, he was an innovator. Charlie Feldman was the first producer to put together the package deal in which he assembled the script, the star(s) and the director for a movie project and then sold the plan to a studio which would then supply financing and distribution services.

Feldman's productions included *The Seven Year Itch, A Streetcar Named Desire, The Group* and *The Glass Menagerie.*

What's New, Pussycat? had originally been a script that Feldman had acquired several years earlier, hoping that Cary

Grant would do it. It's not clear what happened to the script as a possible Cary Grant vehicle but whatever Grant's opinion of it, Charlie decided to have it rewritten. In fact, Feldman had the script rewritten several times, but somehow it never worked out.

Enter Woody Allen. The day after Feldman saw Woody's show at the Blue Angel, he sent a one-man advance scouting party to see what Rollins and Joffe wanted for Woody to rewrite the script. Feldman was prepared to pay $60,000 for the job. He got it for $35,000.

But Woody Allen got a part in the film. And that was apparently the last time that Feldman and Woody agreed about anything.

"I learned something about picture-making," Woody says. "When you're making a big picture for $4,000,000, there are a lot of people around, and they tell you they are *protecting the investment.* They wanted a girl-girl sex-sex picture to make a fortune. I had something else in mind. They got . . . a girl-girl sex-sex picture which made a fortune."

Reduced to its bare bones, the plot of *What's New, Pussycat?* concerns a man who is in love with a girl and wants to marry her, but is afraid to do so because he wants to be faithful to her but isn't sure he can resist other women. A huge variety of beautiful creatures is available to him because of his job as editor of a Paris-based fashion magazine. So he goes to a psychiatrist, hoping to be cured of his lechery.

It's a bright little idea and, in the right hands, could have been a frothy and funny romantic comedy. As Woody Allen has said, "I could have made it twice as funny and half as successful."

Woody told Feldman right off that he didn't think he could do anything to salvage the script he'd been given. Instead, he wrote a new one. At that time, Warren Beatty was slated to play the promiscuous young editor. He didn't like Woody's script and neither did Feldman. So Woody wrote another script.

This one was approved and Feldman began to get the production underway. Murphy's Law—"If anything can go wrong, it probably will!"—was very much in evidence. Warren Beatty refused to appear in the movie because Feldman wouldn't use Leslie Caron, then Beatty's girl friend.

Woody had his own ideas about casting. He very much wanted Groucho Marx to play the part of the psychiatrist. His wish may have been prompted more by nostalgia than by the realities of the young, movie-going audiences in the mid-Sixties. Groucho had always been one of Woody's favorites.

"When I go to a Chaplin movie, I know objectively I'm gonna have a fine experience, but it doesn't thrill me the way the Marx Brothers do. I think Groucho is probably the greatest American comedian.

"There's no heavyweight sense of message. Yet *A Night at the Opera* is more of a commentary on pomposity than anyone could ever be with a gagline about what black-tie society is like," Woody said.

Feldman, however, didn't want Groucho and he had no trouble in signing the man he did want: Peter Sellers. With Sellers as the psychiatrist, Feldman quickly lined up Peter O'Toole as the priapic editor with Romy Schneider as the girl he's in love with. The women out to bed down Peter O'Toole are played by Ursula Andress, Paula Prentiss and Capucine, who was Feldman's girlfriend.

What's New, Pussycat? surely ranks as one of the worst movies ever made. Peter Sellers plays the psychiatrist in a red velvet suit made for an Edwardian schoolboy and a Prince Valiant wig. Given to temper tantrums, sexual attacks on women patients and totally mindless, impulsive behavior, Sellers' Dr. Fritz Fassbinder would not be able to keep a job as an orderly in a mental institution. To accept him as a psychiatrist is impossible.

Peter O'Toole is a puppet of a man without the slightest ability to assess or control his own behavior. And Ursula Andress, Paula Prentiss and Capucine play versions of the male fantasy of women as sex object, suicidal beseecher of male protection and manipulative phony.

The only bright spot in the film is the Romy Schneider character. Except why would such a normal, loving, fresh-faced girl want to marry a loser like O'Toole? Well, stranger things than that have happened in real life, so we'll let that pass. But the film lacks unity. The scenes between O'Toole and Schneider are played fairly straight, i.e. as traditional romantic comedy. But the scenes in which Peter Sellers or Woody Allen appear are farce. Totally lacking in motivation, these scenes are played to get the easy, crude belly laugh. This is okay. The belly laugh is said to be good for the adrenal glands, and in the hands of the Marx Brothers, for instance, farce can attain a certain classic purity of its own. But mixing the two genres—that of romantic comedy and crude farce— just doesn't work. It's like a man trying to impress a woman he's smitten with by telling her the crudest bathroom jokes he knows.

Woody and Charles Joffe left for England in August, 1964, to begin work on the film. Woody had no idea what to expect, which is perhaps just as well. The next few months were a nightmare of indecision and unannounced and sudden changes of plans.

Feldman had hired Clive Donner, a young BBC director, to perform the directorial chores on *Pussycat*. Donner and Woody discussed the script and then began scouting locations. Woody had said from the first that the film should be made in Paris. Feldman wasn't so sure. So Donner and Woody checked out possible sites for filming in Rome and along the French Riviera as well as locations in London and Paris.

This was the first time that Woody Allen had been in Europe. He liked the big cities. The Riviera, however, was not to his taste. "Beach towns make me nervous," he explained. "I cut both knees swimming in the Mediterranean."

Woody had come to Europe with a completed script, but after he had seen some of the locations, he wrote in new scenes and threw away others.

"I came across this remarkable strip joint called The Crazy Horse Cafe. It has some of the most beautiful women in the world. So I wrote a new scene for the movie in which I play their wardrobe man. I plan to spend a week researching the role."

When this bit finally reached the screen it was introduced by Peter O'Toole asking Woody if he had found a job yet.

"Yeah," Woody replies. *"I'm the wardrobe boy at the Crazy Horse. Twenty francs a week."*

"Only four dollars a week?" O'Toole commiserates. *"That's not much money."*

"Yes," Woody says, matter-of-factly, *"but it's all I can afford to pay them."*

After six weeks in London, Woody, Joffe and Donner spent another six weeks in Rome where Feldman had decided they'd make the movie. Woody suddenly found himself a member of the international movie-making set. One night he'd have dinner with Peter O'Toole. The next night it would be William Holden. Woody had to get used to the three-hour Roman dinners that start at 9 p.m. and don't wind up until midnight is approaching.

To pass the time while Feldman made up his mind on numerous details of production, Woody spent many happy hours soaking in what he referred to as Europe's "culture bath." "I've been to every museum and cathedral I could get to," he said. "It's too much art, though. It would be better if I could get it in medium doses over a long period."

And of course Woody Allen had to make the requisite comment on Europe's women. "The English women weren't too pretty, and surprisingly the French, except for some great exceptions, are only fair. But the Italian women are remarkably sexy, because they're broad and dark and don't wear makeup and they look dirty. I mean earthy."

Production still wasn't underway so Woody and Charlie Joffe took off, with Feldman's blessing, for a week of sightseeing in Florence. Woody, all along, had been arguing that the picture should be made in Paris, but had just about given up hope that it would be.

In the middle of their Florence trip, however, Woody and Joffe got a telegram: *Come to Paris immediately. We're going to shoot here.* Woody was delighted that the production was underway and that Paris had been chosen as the location.

The actual filming, though, did not go smoothly. Feldman looked on Woody's script as raw material that he and Donner would shape to Feldman's notion of what the movie ought to be. And Woody didn't like that; it's what made him want to give up writing for television. He wanted more control. Actually, what he wanted was total control.

"It's so unwieldy when you have to work with such a big production; millions of dollars are involved and you have to tailor material for each of the personalities you're working for: Peter O'Toole and Peter Sellers, Romy Schneider and Paula Prentiss. By the time I got it all worked out to everyone's satisfaction, and their agents', and the producer's and my own—that was about fifty per cent of the time—writing *Pussycat* was terribly hard work.

"When Feldman asked me to write the screenplay, he gave me the general theme and told me it had to have a number of women and it had to be in France, and things like that. I had to keep all those elements in mind and work up a script. It's not the kind of thing I would have done if I'd had a free hand, but they offered me a tremendous amount of money to do it. At first we had these meetings and I could see that it wasn't going to be any art movie so I said okay whenever I was asked to change anything. I didn't care. Nobody really knows what they're talking about; the producer says, 'I don't want you to stick to this idea, but let me just tell it to you,' or 'How about shifting that scene from the tail end to the front?' and it all just becomes a mess.

"It was a Marx Brothers kind of script, a crazy script," Woody said, "and their attitude was to crazy it up even more, to get the craziest house and the craziest office and dress everyone in the craziest clothes."

One source of bitter conflict between Feldman and Woody was that Woody wrote far more scenes for himself than Feldman was willing to use. It seems clear that, as Woody originally envisioned his part, his role would have been commensurate with Peter O'Toole's. Before filming began, Woody had told a reporter that *Pussycat* would be about "two Americans and their romantic adventures in Paris."

As shooting progressed, however, Woody's role shrank considerably. "They would say, 'That scene between you and Peter Sellers or you and Peter O'Toole, we're going to let the two Peters do it.' "

Woody's arguments in defense of his original script simply didn't carry any weight in the company he was travelling in. He was a virtual unknown, surrounded by stars and highly experienced wheeler-dealers like Feldman.

"Everybody had more to say than I did," Woody complained. He thought about it. Maybe not *everybody*. "I had more to say than the third assistant propman." But the lines were rigidly drawn. Woody had this to say about his status vis-a-vis that of the second assistant propman: "It was a draw."

"I would like to have directed *Pussycat*," Woody has said.

"I would have made it a funnier movie. I wrote an offbeat script about a hypersexual guy living in Paris and afraid to get married. Establishment people poured money into it. While they managed to retain some of my jokes, they lost 50 per cent of them. But I was happy to have done it because it was my first movie experience. I was just taken off a nightclub stage and made a screenwriter and actor."

Under the grueling pressures of shooting the movie, the long, convivial dinners that Feldman hosted in Rome came to an end. There was too much work to do and there was too much tension generated by the clashing demands of the producer, the actors and the writer.

During the six months that Woody spent in Paris working on *Pussycat*, he ate at the same restaurant every night. His order never varied: filet of sole. As often as not, he'd have to go back to his hotel room and make some changes in the next day's script.

Pussycat was released in June, 1965 and garnered some of the most uncomplimentary reviews in the history of American movie-making. The *New York Times* critic, Bosley Crowther, opened his review with this denunciation:

"Woody Allen, the nightclub comedian, is formally charged with the minor offense of having written what is alleged to be screenplay of "What's New, Pussycat?" But Mr. Allen can deny it, if he wants to, and he is bound to be believed. He can simply state that no one in his right mind could have written this excuse for a script. And no one in his right mind could have directed either, I am sure, although Clive Donner, a respected British director, is charged with being responsible for it."

Crowther goes on to say that it appears as if the actors in *Pussycat* "were allowed to do anything they wanted, say anything they wished, wear any kind of crazy costume, walk out whenever they pleased. And, at the end—maybe the last day of shooting—they were all thrown together in a room and told to try to destroy one another. That's the way it looks."

After describing the movie as "outrageously cluttered and campy, noisy and neurotic", Crowther rhetorically asks, "Why isn't it hearty and hilarious in the manner of an old Marx Brothers farce? . . . I would say because the idea is neurotic and unwholesome, it lacks wit and the actors who are slamming their way through it are not true humorists. Mr. Sellers, the nearest to one, is excessively grotesque and absurd. Mr. O'Toole is too airy and affected, Mr. Allen is too studiously a kook ... And all the way through their labored efforts runs a feeling of psychopathic strain, as though the characters were all disturbed children, engaging in violent, sex-tinged water play."

Bosley Crowther's aim was to apply his own critical standards of taste, intelligence and wit to the movies that crossed his professional path. Charlie Feldman's aim was to make money and he very shrewdly knew that you can get very rich by consistently underestimating the sexual sophistication of mass movie audiences.

In spite of unusually bad reviews, *What's New Pussycat?* grossed more money than any other movie comedy had ever done: between $17 and $20 million.

According to Woody, "Feldman made about two million dollars personally from *Pussycat* and that pleases me very much because he took a chance on me."

Woody also realized that *Pussycat's* fantastic commercial success was "a huge plus for me. It was the big launching pad. Suddenly I could command huge figures ... For all the things I disliked about it, the movie had a certain vitality that people all over the world responded to."

Oddly enough, the movie was not a critical failure everywhere. In Paris, it won an award as "best directed comedy" for 1965. "They're a little crazy there," Woody explained.

Another oddity related to *Pussycat* was that people started confusing the movie's two farceurs, Peter Sellers and Woody Allen. It wasn't just movie fans who would get confused, but people you'd expect to know better—like producers and wives. Peter Sellers was married then to Britt Ecklund.

"She was in bed sick," Woody said, "and the two of us walked into her room. I was first, and she thought I was Peter."

Several months before *Pussycat* opened in New York, Woody couldn't resist planting an item in Leonard Lyons' column in the New York Post:

"Woody Allen studied the cinema in Prof. Robert Gessner's class at NYU and flunked out. Then he enrolled at

CCNY and flunked the movie course there, too. He's just back from Paris, where he wrote and co-starred in What's New, Pussycat? *which cost $4,000,000."*

The success of his first movie project invested Woody Allen with that magical psychological substance known as clout. "I would like to do films, write them, direct them, appear in them," he said about a year after *Pussycat* was released. "Nice modest budgets! Like Jerry Lewis, but much further down the economic scale." Woody was quick to admit that he knew absolutely nothing about directing. "But I think I could direct films in my sleep. It's an inborn thing."

On the basis of *Pussycat*'s success, Feldman offered Woody a small part in his next film: *Casino Royale*, a spoof of the James Bond movies. Allen plays the nephew of 007. The dauntless British agent is played by David Niven, a fairly radical departure from the image of 007 as portrayed by Sean Connery.

Woody's name did not appear on the titles as screenwriter, but several bits in the movie bore his unmistakable comedic flair. In one scene, as Woody faces a firing squad, he pleads, "I have a low threshold of death."

"I wrote that last part of the script, my part, and at first they said it went in a different direction from the rest of the script. Then, months later, they wrote and asked if I had a carbon of the pages I'd sent them because now they were heading in my direction and would reshape the whole script to fit it. They keep rewriting it so much that whenever I tell anyone about my character, it turns out to be something that no longer applies."

Feldman didn't begin shooting *Casino* until nearly eight months after *Pussycat*'s release. In the meantime, Woody had spent the summer and fall of 1965 appearing on television— he was by now a frequent visitor to *The Tonight Show*—and writing: a play (*Don't Drink the Water*), a screenplay (*Take the Money and Run*) and the first of his pieces for *The New Yorker*. In spite of his negative feelings about working on *Pussycat*, he promoted it every chance he got. Joffe had convinced him that only good things could come from being associated with a smash hit.

* * * * * *

For Woody Allen, 1966 was an incredibly successful year. He began it with an engagement at the Americana Hotel's Royal Box. Working his movie-making experiences into his act, Woody summed up his experiences with Ursula Andress, Romy Schneider and Capucine: "Now I fail with a better class of women."

Be that as it may, on February 2, Woody, who had turned 30 the previous December, and Louise Lasser, then 26, were married. There was no honeymoon. Woody went on that night at the Royal Box as usual. He was fond of pointing out that he and Louise had married on Groundhog Day, although he never explained the significance of this timing. He did admit, however, that all his ex-wife jokes "suddenly seemed dated."

He now had a new source of humor: current wife jokes. *"My wife cooked her first dinner for me. I choked on a bone in the chocolate pudding."*

Offstage, however, Woody was unabashedly chivalrous when speaking of Louise. "She's pretty, effervescent, brighter than I am, funnier than I am, intelligent and thoroughly original. She's the only person I ever met who can cheer me up."

Shortly after the wedding, American International, a movie studio with a reputation for making low-budget stinkers that earned very respectable profits, approached Woody with an off-the-wall project.

Hank Saperstein, an American International producer, had bought a Japanese-made film in the James Bond mode. (As movie-makers, the Japanese were no slouches. They knew a good idea when they saw one.) Saperstein wanted Woody to take the film, re-edit it in any fashion he chose and write a new sound track. The movie would be called, *What's Up, Tiger Lily?*, a more than passing reference to Woody's previous hit, *What's New, Pussycat?*

For $75,000 and the chance to do something totally wacky, Woody said yes. "We had a lot of fun doing the movie," he has said. "I got some friends together. (They included Len Maxwell, Frank Buxton, Mickey Rose and Louise.) We went down to Teacher's Sound Studio on Broadway and dubbed in gags and *nonsequiturs* over scenes with all these Japanese people doing strange things.

"It was difficult in some ways, because you'd think of a

great joke for a certain character and it would be three syllables too long to sync with his lip movements."

There were other problems. Woody was still appearing at the Americana. His last show didn't end until 3 a.m. and he had to show up at the sound studio by 8 a.m. because the budget for *Tiger Lily* did not allow for overtime for the engineers.

The movie tells the story of Phil Moscowitz, "lovable rogue", and his search for a certain recipe for egg salad. Success in this search is almost unbearably crucial because "it is written that he who has the best recipe for egg salad shall rule over heaven and earth."

Moscowitz and his cohorts are pursued by mystifying assortments of thugs. These guys are real baddies. "They kill, they maim, and not only that, they call information for numbers they could easily look up themselves."

Along this basic "plot" line, gush a constant stream of one-liners:

Two henchmen are hungrily watching a stripper hard at work in a dingy bistro.

"Isn't she fantastic?" No. 1 asks.

"She was even better in Sound of Music,*"* No. 2 says.

* * * * * *

The barely clothed heroine is relaxing in Phil's apartment after a seemingly miraculous jailbreak.

"I wonder who arranged my escape," she broods. *"I had an idea it was the Mormon Tabernacle Choir—but they have no motive."*

* * * * * *

Phil gets the drop on the bad guys. *"You'd better not mess around with me unless you're completely unashamed of your bodies,"* he snaps.

* * * * * *

Phil and several of his sexy female agents are captured. An endless stream of hired guns pour in the door. The head crook sighs. *"Everybody shows up when we have girls to tie up,"* he moans.

* * * * * *

Finally, the decisive gun battle is underway. But Phil is out of ammunition. He turns to the audience: *"If enough of you believe in fairies my gun will be magically filled with bullets."*

* * * * * *

Enough of us must have believed, because the bullets appear where needed.

In a brief prologue to the film, Woody appeared on screen and said what he had done with *Tiger Lily* wasn't really that unusual. The first use of this technique, he explained, was in *Gone with the Wind*. This classic film was actually "a Japanese movie with Southern voices dubbed in."

Tiger Lily was considered a delicious bit of wacked-out humor by those audiences that were hip and urban and sophisticated enough to understand and laugh at all its injokes, most of which depended on a fairly wide and cynical knowledge of current cultural and media cliches.

Needless to say, *Tiger Lily* never approached *Pussycat* in its box-office gross.

* * * * * *

That fall was frantic. Woody and Louise were in the process of moving to a duplex in a brownstone on 79th Street just off Park Avenue. Woody was in London to shoot *Casino Royale* and commuting back to Manhattan every week-end to oversee casting and other details for his play, *Don't Drink the Water*, which David Merrick was producing on Broadway.

Woody had begun writing the play during his nightclub years at the request of Broadway producer Max Gordon who, like movie producer Charlie Feldman, was an early and instant admirer of Woody's work. It took Woody nearly two years to complete this first play, originally entitled *Yankee, Come Home*.

Unfortunately, Gordon did not think it good enough to warrant production. Woody then asked David Merrick to read the play. Merrick's opinion was favorable. He told Woody he'd produce *Yankee* for the 1966 season.

The play had its share of pre-opening disasters. Merrick wanted Vivian Vance to play the female lead. Woody had written the play as a kind of Jewish family situation comedy. He considered Vance a good actress and fine comedienne but simply too WASP-y to play the Jewish wife that Woody envisioned. Merrick's wishes prevailed, however, and Vance was signed.

Robert B. Sinclair, a former Broadway director who'd recently been working in television in Los Angeles, had been Max Gordon's choice of director and Woody kept him on.

By the time the play opened for tryout in Philadelphia, its title had become *Don't Drink the Water*. The plot revolved around a New Jersey family—mother, father, daughter—who accidentally become enmeshed in a major political crisis while vacationing in an unnamed Iron Curtain country. Complications arise from the measures taken by the American Embassy to extricate them from their predicament.

"My main difficulty in writing a play for the first time is to make sure that the audience doesn't stop laughing," Woody said. These innocent words were spoken six months before the play opened. In spite of his frustrating experiences during the filming of *Pussycat*, Woody had apparently forgotten that a project involving other people has far more potential for disaster than, say, writing a three or four page casual for *The New Yorker* or working out a new routine for himself to use at the Royal Box or the Bitter End.

The opening in Philadelphia drew a mixed response from the critics, although the audiences were laughing. But the production wasn't drawing big enough audiences and Woody felt the play "was falling apart. It was a non-directed play."

Sinclair was replaced by Stanley Prager. Woody continued rewriting and the play was re-staged. But tension among the company was high. The actors would get line changes at noon for a one p.m. matinee. This is a practice severely frowned upon by most actors. Still, they usually remembered their new lines, and somehow the play struggled on. But no one was certain it would ever reach New York.

Merrick had hinted that he might put it in a theatre in Florida (!) until it was in good enough shape for the Big Apple.

Reflecting this frenetic and uncertain period is a hilarious interview that Woody gave to a New York columnist during the Philly tryouts. For the careful reader, it helps explain a basic reaction of Woody Allen's nature, i.e. the worse things get, the more you joke about them.

When asked what the play was about, Woody said, "It has to do with three men on a raft in the Pacific and the various things that happen to them in the middle of the ocean. Of course, there's a terrific set problem which we haven't fully solved.

"Designer Jo Mielziner, I think, is going to solve it by immersing the audience in water. Then, too, we have the problem that the play has only three characters but 23 speaking parts. This, I believe, is a challenge to the ingenuity of the director.

"And of course, there's another story line that runs through the whole thing. It involves this atomic scientist who is confronted with a moral issue. He kills himself in the first two minutes of the play and the rest of the story features doors opening and closing, like in an old Marx Brothers picture, but nobody goes in or out!

"In addition to this," Woody continued, "part of the action centers around a man whose father dies mysteriously, and his father's brother marries the widow, but the father appears to his son in a vision and tells him to avenge the murder. The boy procrastinates, however, and ultimately dies himself in a series of very tragic killings.

"Then there's the counterplot about black market selling in wartime, about how in the French underground they're selling black market medicine. And there's a lot of killing and raping and looting, all of which culminates in a musical finale."

"There's never a moment the play isn't on my mind," Woody said in a more serious vein. "Why only yesterday, noticing that some scenes moved slowly, I took all the alternate pages out of the script. Now the action moves much more swiftly."

A number of philosophers and psychologists have declared a connection, albeit underground and hidden, between hostility and humor. Woody's remarks about Merrick give much credence to that theory.

"Although I wrote the play in four hours—the first two of which were used to think up the plot—I've had to spend a great deal of energy dealing with the producer, David Merrick. He took the play within 48 hours after I gave it to him, but since then he and I have had ever so many tiring details to work out.

"For instance, Mr. Merrick is giving me no author's percentage. Instead, I get the orange juice and Hershey bar concessions in the theaters. I didn't want this, but Mr. Merrick is stronger than I am. Then, too, he made me drive the cast to Philadelphia. And, to calm my nerves, he's agreed to let me have his barbering rights. I get to fix his mustache every morning.

"I don't care *what* they say about Mr. Merrick," Woody loyally declared. "To me, he's Santa Claus—with a Luger."

* * * * * *

The production moved to Boston for more tryouts. Even though he was ill, Woody kept rewriting and Prager started making cast changes . . . a great many cast changes. The role of the daughter was played by four actresses before Prager and Woody were satisfied; the ambassador was played by three actors before one of them clicked.

The most important cast change in Woody's opinion was replacing Vivian Vance with Kay Medford. Suddenly, he said, the wife became "a hilarious character."

And that, of course, is what Woody was after: as many laughs as possible. "I would love to write a sophisticated comedy like one of George S. Kaufman's. I want to write something that is basically human and has funny lines as well. I don't want to write anything deep; I want to amuse people and please them while they're in the theatre.

"You know, everyone has a tendency to equate the fact that I'm successful with the idea that I have a command of things. But it's not true. I happen to have been born with a specific talent that's commercial, through no fault or great enterprise of my own. It just so happens that instead of my being able to write Wagnerian operas which don't sell a damn, I can make people laugh and that's a very commercial commodity. Salaries are insane. A policeman who stands in the streets in the freezing cold risking his life gets almost nothing, and I go on Ed Sullivan and talk for a few minutes and make thousands of dollars. But I'm inept in my private life, in my marriages, filmmaking, playwriting—everything.

"What saves me all the time from complete disaster is that there is a talent underneath. Look at my first play, *Don't Drink the Water*. I didn't know anything about writing a play, but I wrote it. We made twelve cast changes—the most in history for a straight play out of town—and fired the director. I was sick with a 102° temperature. It was utter bedlam; the play was going down the drain. But when it finally opened in New York, it was undeniably funny."

Opening night at the Morosco Theatre finally arrived. Woody watched most of the first act. Lou Jacobi had been in the part of the husband from the very beginning and now he and Kay Medford were bouncing their lines off each other wonderfully. Feeling enormous relief that the laughs were all coming at the right places, Woody decided to walk off a bad case of the fidgets with Mickey Rose. He also wanted to avoid any demands for the author to appear at curtain call time, a Broadway custom on opening night.

Woody and Mickey slipped out of the theatre before the first act curtain. They wandered up Eighth Avenue, ending up at McGirr's Billiard Academy, an establishment right out of a Damon Runyon short story.

After shooting some pool, they went down to the Automat at 46th and Broadway and had macaroni and pumpkin pie for dinner. "Some nice people who looked like bookies came over and wished me good luck," Woody reported.

Later, Woody heard that, in one scene, Lou Jacobi had gestured so hard that one of his cuff links flew into the orchestra seats. When Woody saw Jacobi the next day at the Russian Tea Room, he said, "We can't have that happen again. It slows up the action. So go out and get your wrists pierced."

The critics did not wholeheartedly praise the play; they had many complaints about the lack of a sufficiently complex comedic situation and they observed that the play showed its origins in night club comedy in its exhausting excess of unmotivated one-liners. But generally the reviews were favorable.

Audiences loved the play and lined up to buy tickets long enough to give *Don't Drink the Water* an 18-month run.

A few weeks after the play opened, Woody signed a contract with Caesar's Palace in Las Vegas. It was his first appearance in the Nevada gambling capital.

On December 1, 1966, Woody Allen turned 31 and discovered that he was a solidly successful comedian, scenarist, playwright, actor and contributor to *The New Yorker*.

He and Louise were now settled into their duplex in a brownstone on 79th Street near Park Avenue. Louise, who had been Barbra Streisand's understudy in *I Can Get It for You Wholesale*, was getting more and more work in television commercials.

Woody had worked up an appropriately daft account of their courtship. "We met when I was free-fall parachuting and she passed me. But I was struck by her beauty and I caught up to her. Later, we were married in space by a rabbi who was free-falling, too."

Woody and Louise, however, may have had a slightly different notion of what settling into a new house involved than your average young, upwardly mobile East Side couple. Louise has said they lived in the big apartment "like two kids in a castle." All the decisions concerning the house were left to the housekeeper.

One room had nothing but a billiard table in it. "I noodle around," Woody explained. "I'm a surprisingly bad player for someone who owns a table. I may be the worst owner-player."

Another handsome, wood-paneled room held nothing but a jukebox (a Wurlitzer, it remained unplugged) and an electric organ. An Emil Nolde watercolor and an Oscar Kokoscha drawing remained on the floor, leaning against the wall, for months. Woody had bought both works with his poker winnings during the London filming of *Casino Royale*.

Three oils by Gloria Vanderbilt also waited to be hung as well as a few of Woody's own efforts on canvas. "Painting is another thing I do badly," he said. All of Woody's paintings have "autumn" in the title. One that he had named "Autumn

Camel" showed a grinning television screen, a camel and "either a Dutch boy or a toadstool."

Before he and Louise were married, he had lived in a two-room apartment at 74th and Park. At that time, he had yearned for a bigger place. "I'd like something where somebody could be in another part of the apartment and get murdered, and I wouldn't even know about it."

The new apartment was certainly better than the old one, but it had many flaws. "I feel good (about it)," Woody said. "But not *that* good. Because it's big enough that an assault could go on, and certainly blackmail, without my knowing about it, but I'm still not sure about murder."

The scarcity of furniture in the new apartment meant that Woody had plenty of room for his collection of magician's equipment. "I've had extensive magical apparatus my whole life," Woody said. "I find—this is one of those meaningless observations I frequently make—that comedians often have side interests that revolve around goods, like magic or photography or musical instruments. As I said, it's an absolutely useless observation."

But of course it isn't What is more ephemeral than laughter? What is more difficult to define than humor? What makes us laugh at one absurdity and not another? Not even the founder of modern depth psychology, Sigmund Freud, was able to extract the essence of humor in his long essay on the subject. It's not surprising, therefore, that the men and women who make their living at this uncertain and evanescent craft should occasionally take comfort in getting their hands on something *real*.

In 1966, Woody Allen wrote and edited a movie (*What's Up, Tiger Lily?*), appeared in and partially wrote another (*Casino Royale*), saw his first play reach Broadway (*Don't Drink the Water*), began showing up regularly in the pages of *The New Yorker*, appeared at Americana Hotel's Royal Box in New York and at Caesar's Palace in Las Vegas. His take for the year came to over $250,000. Happily, he had a tax expert in the family. Louise's father was S. Jay Lasser, a man who'd been advising the American taxpayer for decades.

Woody admits to a certain carelessness with his dollars. "I like to spend it foolishly for things I enjoy—I'd like to have a

Monet, but $175,000 is still too much. However, I don't worry about it or even think about it.

"I'm not a beatnik, though, by any construction. I like opulent surroundings if at all possible.

"Success hasn't changed me much. I feel a little more self-confident, I suppose, but that's about all. Except that now I live in a six-room duplex on Park Avenue. But I still don't have enough space. When you move into a big apartment, each room becomes something. You have a dining room, a living room, a game room. But there's no room for a maid to sleep in. It's not like it was when you lived in a smaller place and you had rooms that doubled for different purposes.

"I get a lot of phone calls and mail from people who want to tell me that they have had things happen to them that are just like the things that happen to me. One girl named Natalie left word with my answering service that she had to speak to me, it was terribly urgent. I tried to call her back and when I finally got her on the telephone, she stammered and said, 'Oh, I never thought you would call me. I just don't have anything to say to you!' "

* * * * * *

As always when he was working out of town, Woody took his clarinet, his KLH portable stereo and a sampling of his collection of New Orleans jazz records with him when he left New York for the year-end gig at Caesar's Palace. In spite of his poker skills, Woody Allen is basically not a gambler. Since there's virtually no sightseeing in Las Vegas, Woody spent his time during the day holed up in his room, sitting in with the Dixieland greats who performed on his records. "You could say I'm bad but devoted," Woody says.

Back in New York, Woody and Louise decided to throw a New Year's Eve party. At first, according to N.Y. Post columnist Earl Wilson, the plan was to turn the apartment into a discotheque, complete with topless waitresses.

Then the plans were changed.

"I discussed it with my wife, Louise, whom I married Ground Hog's Day. She said either they went or I went," Woody said. "We decided *not* to have topless waitresses."

Woody and Louise naively figured tht lots of people were giving New Year's Eve parties. So they told the friends they'd invited to bring *their* friends. The result was total bedlam.

"It was fantastic," Woody said. "What started as a small party—we told everyone to bring their friends because we thought no one would come—turned into a thing with 500 people. We had expected maybe 250. I've got the whole thing on camera because I set up a television camera at the front door to photograph the arrivals. It was unbelievable.

"In the middle of the party, I had to send out for seven cases of liquor. It didn't stop. There was a line down the stairs and out onto the street waiting to get in. People just kept coming. It cost me thousands of dollars more than I had expected. At one point, it became frightening. All those people. So my wife and I left. We just went down to the corner and had a sandwich at the drugstore. We had to get out of there.

"But there was surprisingly little damage," Woody said. "And the next day one of our neighbors found our Matisse drawing on the stairs and returned it."

In a year-end interview, a reporter asked Woody if his success wasn't threatening to trap him in a life of increasing respectability?

Woody demurred. "There are half-a-dozen things not considered respectable by any cultural group anywhere in the world that I'd like to do. The most I can tell you is that one of them has to do with a giraffe. It would take more courage than I have to tell you more."

But on another issue, he simply had to agree: "I guess this *has* been a good year."

* * * * * *

Most people would have celebrated such a year with a Caribbean cruise, a few weeks at St. Moritz or, at the very least, taken a month just to goof off. Not Woody Allen. Early in 1967, he began writing the screenplay that would become *Take the Money and Run*, the first film over which he had complete control and *Play It Again, Sam*, which would become his second Broadway play and later a movie that he would write and star in with Diane Keaton.

"I like to goof around . . . but if I'm not creating something funny after half a day goes by I start to feel guilty. You know, if I couldn't do it anymore, it would be a spectacular pleasure to be a bum. Just walk through the park, maybe go to a movie, watch TV. I could get a part-time job but I couldn't see myself working at a regular job. I wouldn't be *able* to do that, to spend all that time just working. It would be terrible."

But "just working" is what Woody Allen, by his own admission, spends most of his time doing. Fifteen-hour writing days in the little office next to his bedroom are not uncommon. "I just can't stop myself," Woody has said. "If I went to Jamaica for two weeks, after an hour there I would begin to get nervous because time is passing and I'm not writing.

"When I write I like to put down everything that comes into my head, anything at all—wild monkeys!—and then rewrite as I go along. I work on a typewriter although when I work on one of my monologues, I run around the room and holler to myself—I never write those out, I just jot the ideas down on paper.

"I function well in comedy. It's an odd sort of peculiarity. Some people can paint. Some can act. How many people can make up jokes? Such a wild talent! Like a trampoline artist. To be funny on stage or in print is a wonderful talent. It's hard for me not to be funny. It's hard for me not to be ridiculous.

"The only important thing for a comedian to be is funny. There's a tendency to take comedy too seriously these days. Suddenly, articles about comedians are appearing in magazines like *Encounter*. There's nothing a comedian can teach me about philosophy or art or religion. When comedians succeed, they succeed because they're funny.

"All the people I adore are what you'd call aggressive wits. I'm not and it kills me . . . I'd like to be a 'hostile' comedian, like Fields or Groucho. Those are the ones I admire. But that's not me. And I'm not a social critic either. I guess that just doesn't interest me. I like to read philosophy, but not social criticism."

* * * * * *

Woody Allen had become a show-biz phenomenon and offers—to write, to direct, to perform—poured in. Among them was a query from MGM. Would Allen be interested in directing Robert Morse in a comedy to be called, *Don Quixote, U.S.A.* Woody said no, he didn't like the script.

"I don't need the work, so I can wait until I can do something worthwhile where I have complete control," Woody said.

In addition to writing *Take the Money and Run* and *Play It Again, Sam*, Woody was also working out a number of new routines for his next appearance at the Americana Hotel's Royal Box.

He opened there in May . . . for $9,000 a week and a percentage of the gross. Introduced as "sportsman and spoiler of women," Woody's act indicated that writing in more sophisticated genres had definitely not stopped his apparently inexhaustible supply of one-liners.

* * * * * *

"I've been busy writing a non-fiction version of the Warren Report."

"You know, David Merrick is one of my favorite producers. Another one is John Wilkes Booth. If the Nazis were after me and I was hiding in a closet, David would tell them where I was, even if they didn't ask him."

"My parents had my baby shoes bronzed. Unfortunately, my feet were still in them."

"It's very embarrassing to be sitting with a girl in the Stork Club and have her arrested by Israeli agents."

* * * * * *

In spite of the fact that Woody and Louise had been married for nearly a year and a half now, Woody still had the full complement of ex-wife jokes in his act. Harlene, through an attorney, had made it plain that she wanted them to stop. She threatened a lawsuit. Woody kept the ex-wife jokes in the act.

Two months later, in July, 1967, Harlene filed a $1 million defamation of character suit in Manhattan Supreme Court. She named NBC as co-defendant, citing material that Woody had used on *The Tonight Show* and on *The Perry Como Show*. Harlene claimed that Allen's jokes had held her up to "scorn and ridicule".

She cited various examples:

"I should have known something was wrong when I took her home. My parents approved, but my dog died."

"My first wife had that change-of-sex operation six times. They couldn't come up with anything she liked."

* * * * * *

In contrast, Woody's relationship with wife #2, Louise Lasser, seemed ideal. Before their marriage, Woody Allen had said, "I don't consider any girl perfect unless she rejects me." Then he explained how Louise orchestrated their marriage: "Louise manages to achieve a brilliant kind of thing. She accepts me and at the same time manages to hold me at arm's length. She keeps me insecure, off balance at times. She accepts me—at a bare minimum for the relationship."

Woody's sister, Letty, was now 23. Unlike Woody, she had made it through Brooklyn College and was now married to a psychologist and working as a schoolteacher.

Woody's father, Martin Konigsberg, now had his own engraving shop (jewelry, not money) on Eldridge Street in Manhattan. Dominating the shop's windows were posters of Woody's play, *Don't Drink the Water*. Every day after work Martin would take the subway up to the Morosco and buy tickets to his son's play.

"My customers ask me to buy them," Martin explained. "Every night I go up to the box office to get them. An accommodation. Since the show opened in November, they bought $11,000 worth. I got orders for three months ahead. The tickets aren't even printed yet."

Woody had recently bought his parents an apartment in Manhattan only five blocks from his own place. He and Louise visited the Konigsbergs at least once a week.

In addition to his satisfaction at Woody's professional success, Martin Konigsberg also said he was very proud of the friendship that existed between Woody and Letty, unusual in that Woody was nine years older than his sister.

"They talk for hours on the phone," Martin said. "Woody

always tries out his comedy on his sister first. But they won't tell me one gag. They call it 'Classified Information.' "

Woody would go on walks around Manhattan with Martin and discuss his latest projects and offers with his father. Martin no doubt remembered his former despair over this boy of his who used to cut school to go to the movies. "Now they pay him $10,000 for eight minutes on TV," Martin observed, "and little fortunes for plays and movies."

The only distractions on Woody's strolls about the city with his father were literary. "On every walk," Martin said, "we pass a bookstore and he runs in and buys five, six at a time. How that boy reads! He reads everything."

Martin confessed that Woody had sent his parents on several splendid vacations and that all Martin had to do was brush off his suit and Woody would insist on buying him two new ones.

"He's always generous," said Martin. "More important, he's a nice man. But he's always ribbing me. He tells all my friends he was kidnapped when he was a kid and I fell asleep reading the ransom note and as soon as I woke up I rented his room."

* * * * * *

By the fall of 1967, Woody had completed writing *Play It Again, Sam*. It was scheduled for production during the 1967-68 theatre season. Unfortunately, there were complications. "I wrote for myself," Woody said, "and I'm not available."

Woody Allen might well have cited his unavailability (to himself yet!) as further proof of the legendary Woody Allen incompetence: "My life... is a series of botches and bungles, and it's only that. In the end, the jokes keep me afloat. Off-stage, I'm very serious. I'm not a joker, but the point is I can't *not* see the funny side of things. Comedy occurs to me. I don't make any effort for it, it's just the natural way I think. That kind of thing shakes people because they want to believe there's something you can positively work on. For me, especially, it's just bungling through."

Instead of shepherding *Sam* onto Broadway, Woody had to spend the last several months of 1967 producing, writing and starring in his own television special on NBC.

Woody had long considered television a "prissy" medium that unreasonably restricted a writer's freedom. "We shouldn't do this. Don't mention that. Tone this down. Don't get into trouble . . . I've been censored on the blandest things. Once I used a phrase, rhythmic birth control, and they bleeped out the word 'rhythmic'.

"Another time," Woody continued, "I did a routine about being beaten up in an alley, and in describing it I said, 'I used the old Navajo Indian trick, screaming and yelling.' Don't you know they worried about me offending the Navajos?"

The ostensible subject of the upcoming *Kraft Music Hall* comedy hour was to be a news review of 1967. This would be an especially difficult assignment for Woody since he always made a point of *not* being a topical comedian.

"I have an aversion to topicality," Woody declared. "It has always been my opinion that comedians get off too easily mouthing current events or popular name brands. And it's not very funny. There's nothing worse than yesterday's news. Besides, this kind of comedy doesn't stand up. I have a monologue on one of my record albums that's 2½ years old, and it's still listened to.

"TV is important—in a commercial way—so that the performer can function artistically. But it isn't on a level with motion pictures or the stage. But for an occasional appearance—well, that audience is vast . . . vast.

"I'm constantly being offered TV series," Woody said. "And so far they've all been mediocre to the core. Nowhere is there any real excitement, or a sense of unpredictability . . ."

In order to generate a sense of unpredictability on his show and perhaps to give at least the aura of topicality to the proceedings, Woody asked conservative author and publisher William F. Buckley to appear. "I think he'll offer good contrast to me," Woody said.

Also appearing on the show were singer Aretha Franklin and actress Liza Minnelli. The high point of comedy hour was Liza and Woody doing their interpretation of *Bonnie and Clyde*, which had been *the* movie of the year starring Faye Dunaway and Warren Beatty.

Woody no doubt wanted to put himself into a criminal

frame of mind because the next item on his agenda was a very important one: his very own movie, the first time he would have complete artistic control from the first to the last frame of film. And in *Take the Money and Run* Woody Allen was fulfilling, albeit in fantasy, his boyhood dream of being a master criminal.

"I thought it would be very satisfying to be a good burglar—it takes great planning and thought, you know. Crime . - . ." Woody mused, "you make your own hours. It's creative work. It's lucrative work. The *only* drawback—it's dangerous." He paused and thought for a moment and suddenly seemed to gain a fresh insight: "How much more dangerous is it than land speculation?" The question hung, unanswered, in the air.

"The movie is autobiographical in that it's about a pathological criminal," Woody said, in his best deadpan put-on manner. "There was a period when I seriously considered being a criminal. I used to read a tremendous amount about crime. I knew everything about jails and robberies. I knew the names of all the gangsters. The way kids list the best all-star teams, I would make lists of the five best guys to knock over a bank."

"I think I would have made the kind of criminal you'll see in this film," Woody said earnestly. "I never would have stopped trying to beat the law in the face of persistent defeat."

Woody also said that *Take the Money and Run* would have other facets. "It's a vehicle for my many talents: my exploits with women, my imitation of Gov. Alfred E. Smith and my work on the trampoline."

* * * * * *

Movie-making is, in addition to its glamourous aspects, a gruelling, time-consuming, nit-picking business. As director, Woody had to attend to dozens of technical details he had never before extensively dealt with: lighting, locations, set and costume design, script continuity, hiring the various crews. He spent most of 1968 dealing with these problems. By the time he had everything worked out to his satisfaction and was ready to begin shooting, it was September and the year was three-fourths gone.

Three memorable and hilarious films which
Woody directed and starred in were *Take
the Money and Run* (above left), *Love and
Death* (above right) and *Sleeper*.

The private Woody is an accomplished musician and an avid basketball
fan who is no mean dribbler himself. He and second wife Louise
Lasser are shown shortly after their marriage on Groundhog Day, 1966.

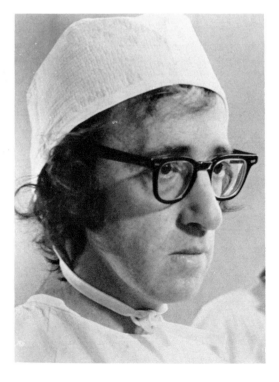

In *The Front* (above), which starred Woody, but which he did not direct, his
generally anti-establishment political posture found a frank, even heroic out-
let. *Annie Hall* was compared by *New York Times* critic Vincent Canby to
the work of Ingmar Bergman. In the scene below, Woody confronts his
childhood self (played by Jonathan Munk) reacting to the world of struc-
tured education. In real life Woody was just as negative.

Two uncharacteristic moments in Woody's life were his presentation to Britain's Queen Elizabeth and his escorting of First Lady Betty Ford to a party honoring Martha Graham. In the first instance, Woody appears in a reverse Oreo pose between Ursula Andress and Raquel Welch, while in the second he stayed true to himself by wearing sneakers with his tuxedo.

Lovers, good friends, and the most popular comedy team since Tracy and Hepbur
the Allen-Keaton relationship remains as hard to define as it ever
was since being immortalized in *Annie Hall.*

Take the Money and Run tells, in the old *March of Time* documentary style, of Virgil Starkwell, a mild-mannered, myopic and inept criminal. (Virgil *has* to be inept; he was created and played by Woody Allen. If Virgil weren't inept, he wouldn't be funny.)

Virgil's first criminal caper takes place when he is a mere boy. He tries to rob a gumball machine. Unfortunately, his hand gets stuck in the slot and he is captured.

Virgil's first prison break as a young man should have been a momentous occasion. He carefully carves a pistol out of a bar of soap. He covers his sculpture with black shoe polish. Virgil's creation is so lethal in appearance that he handles it gingerly lest the gun go off in his cell. The moment arrives and Virgil herds two guards ahead of him across the prison yard. Unfortunately, there's a fierce downpour and just before they unlock the gates, the guards turn around to observe that Virgil's gun has become a mass of soapsuds.

Virgil's first big-time bank robbery was much more carefully planned. Unfortunately, the teller can't make out all the words on the note that Virgil pushes across the counter.

TELLER: What does this say?

VIRGIL: Can't you read it?

TELLER: I . . . can't read this. What's this? Act natural?

VIRGIL: No. It says: Please put fifty thousand dollars into this bag and act natural.

TELLER: It does *say "act natural".*

VIRGIL: (makes a point of looking at the note) "I am pointing a gun at you."

TELLER: That looks like gub, that doesn't look like gun.

VIRGIL: (looks at the note with the teller) No, that . . . that's gun.

TELLER: No, that gub . . . that's a "b".

VIRGIL: No. That's an "n". That's gun.

TELLER: (gets the attention of another teller) George, would you step over here a moment, please? What does this say?

GEORGE: "Please put fifty thousand dollars into this bag and abt natural." What's "abt".

VIRGIL: "Act"!

TELLER: (Ignoring Virgil.) Does this . . . does this look like "gub" or "gun"?

GEORGE: *"Gun", see? But what does "abt" mean?*
VIRGIL: *"Act". That's "act natural." It says, "Please put fifty thousand dollars into this bag and act natural."*
TELLER: *Oh, I see. This is a hold-up.*
VIRGIL: *Yes.*
TELLER: *May I see your gun?*
VIRGIL: *Oh. (He opens his jacket to show the gun stuck under his belt.)*
TELLER: *Well, you'll have to have this note initialed by one of our vice-presidents before I can give you any money.*
VIRGIL: *Please. I'm in a rush.*
TELLER: *I'm sorry, but that's our policy. (He points.) The gentleman in the gray suit.*

But the vice-president has trouble deciphering the note, also, and soon everyone in the bank is arguing over what Virgil's note really says. And when they finally figure it out, it means that Virgil is on his way back to prison.

His love life is marred by similar mix-ups. Walking in the park, Virgil sees a girl sitting on the grass, gazing dreamily into space. His first plan is to steal her purse, but he falls in love with her instead: *"After 15 minutes, I wanted to marry her. After 30 minutes, I'd completely given up the idea of snatching her purse."*

Louise, played by Janet Margolin, makes her living as a laundress: *"I like my work but I don't find it very interesting."* After she and Virgil are married, the unkind suspicion arises in the viewer's mind that perhaps Louise is not playing the game of life with a full deck at her disposal.

She pours boiling coffee over Virgil's teabag. She leaves the cellophane wrapping intact when she cooks Virgil's steak. There is, of course, an explanation for Louise's flakiness. She was an adopted child in a broken home. Her father was a career Army man who, after 30 years in the service, "catapulted to corporal". Louise's adoptive mother was an alcoholic who regularly held conversations with God "about religion and interior decorating."

"This picture is such a dichotomy", Woody said. "It's got this pastoral love story. Janet is so pastoral, she's a virginal D.W. Griffith heroine. And I'm this cheesy punk hoodlum."

Most of the exteriors were shot in or near San Francisco,

one of the few cities besides New York that Woody Allen feels comfortable in.

Janet Margolin had her first big success as an actress when she played, at 18, the disturbed heroine in the 1961 film *David and Lisa*. She said that *Take the Money and Run* was the first movie she had enjoyed making since her work in *David and Lisa*. "It's my first grown-up role," Janet said. "I don't object to playing sweet girls if it's something with meat on it. But I never did a comic role before. I'm playing a girl who's funny. Woody thinks I'm beautifully and hysterically funny and I'm having the time of my life. We work together so fantastically, you won't believe it. We improvise every scene."

"We have been an unremitting source of delight to ourselves," Woody said, "and if this movie could break even on two tickets, we'd do all right.

"I don't know the first thing about directing," Woody added. "So I showed the crew some movies I like in order to explain the abstract feelings I have in a concrete way."

These "model" films included *Blow-Up* (for its color), *Elvira Madigan* (for its sense of sweetness), *Live for Life* (for sex education . . . another Woody Allen put-on, perhaps?), *I Was a Fugitive from a Chain Gang* (Virgil spends time on a chain gang during one of his stints in prison) and *The Eleanor Roosevelt Story* (for documentary quality).

Woody said that he did not show films by Bergman and Bunuel, whose works affect him deeply, because the basic thrust of their work is so different from his. "They could only be a bad influence on me because they're so antithetical to comedy. Bergman interests me more than anyone because of the consummate marriage of technique, theatricality and themes that are both personally important to me and that have gigantic size—death, the meaning of life, the question of religious faith. No religion in the world interests me, but *speculation* on religious matters does interest me. Bunuel has the same contempt for religion as it has come down to us that I have. he has the key to me somehow, although his themes don't interest me as much as Bergman's because he takes them from a more sociological viewpoint . . ."

When *Take the Money and Run* was finally released in

August, 1969, it was most often described as an extended visual monologue, a la Woody Allen, stand-up comedian. *The New York Times* reviewer said: "Like a nightclub monologue, the movie has a sort of loose-leaf form. You have a feeling that scenes and, perhaps, entire reels could be taken out and rearranged without making much difference in total impact, which is good because it all looks so effortless."

"I have to regard this first film strictly as a learning process," Woody said. "I think there will be 100 per cent improvement in the second."

By the time *Take the Money and Run* was unreeling on U.S. movie screens, Woody Allen had already been onstage for months in *Play It Again, Sam*. Playing opposite him was a relatively unknown young actress named Diane Keaton.

chapter 4

Hollywood
and Broadway:
Fulfilled Ambitions

DIANE KEATON'S CHILDHOOD was as different from Woody
Allen's as a hush puppy is different from gefilte fish. Born in
Los Angeles, she grew up in nearby Santa Ana, the oldest of
four children. The three daughters and one son of Jack Hall
and Dorothy Keaton grew up in a typical California tract
house. Diane says her civil engineer father, who now runs his
own consulting firm, was a public employee during her
childhood and only became "very successful late in life."

Diane spent her childhood vacillating between terrible
bouts of shyness and an equally intense need to stand out, to
be noticed, to be recognized. She sang in the Methodist
Church choir, tried out for school plays, tried out for cheer-
leader and in high school, tried to look different by wearing
white lipstick and black net stockings.

In her senior year, she landed the second lead in the Santa
Ana High School production of *Little Mary Sunshine.* It
proved to be a seductive experience. "I sang my solo and then
I was backstage, and I heard this sound. And then I couldn't
believe it. It was applause, and they were clapping for me, and
it was *so loud.*"

She spent a couple of semesters each at several small
California colleges. She went "for the musicals" and ap-

parently there weren't enough of them to suit her taste. On the advice of her high school acting teacher, she came to New York and began studying at Manhattan's Neighborhood Playhouse School of the Theatre.

Several years later, she had achieved little more than a few small parts in summer stock productions. After months of trying out and getting nowhere, she turned up at the auditions for *Hair*. Here, too, she was dismissed.

Thoroughly discouraged, she waited for a backstage elevator. "Man, did I feel bad. I mean, I felt bad. I was thinking 'This is ridiculous.' "

Then one of the producers, a Frenchman, happened by and noticed her.

"No, you stay," he said.

"I have no idea why he decided to keep me," Diane says.

But, at 22, she was on her way.

Her first assignment in *Hair* was to understudy the star, Lynn Kellogg. Then Kellogg left the show and Keaton took over her role. (Remember *Good Morning, Starshine*? It was Keaton's big number, a joyous and oddly vulnerable song.)

Unlike the rest of the cast, Keaton declined to shed her clothes for the bare-assed finale, although she freely admits taking long peeks at her fellow actors. "I was quite curious . . . I mean, I wouldn't say I was *not* curious, you know? I mean, I took a look or two, sure."

Keaton's overwhelming feeling during her *Hair* period, however, was not curiosity about her fellow actors' anatomies but insecurity about her own future. "I was living alone on the West Side, in a one-room apartment with the bathroom out in the hallway and the bathtub in the kitchen, right? I didn't feel like I had arrived with *Hair*. That play wasn't much for individual performances."

When she heard that auditions were being held for a new play by Woody Allen she called Joe Hardy, the director, and said she'd like to read for the female lead. Hardy had to tell her that the biggest woman's role in the play wasn't a plum; she'd play the wife of Woody's best friend. All the rest of the female roles were little more than walk-ons. That's okay, Keaton said. She was still interested.

Woody Allen and Joe Hardy like her right away. But they

had committed themselves to auditioning nearly 50 actresses. Finally, Diane was called back to audition with Woody.

"He was as scared as I was," Keaton recalls. "And I thought he was great—I'd seen him on television before and I thought he was real cute—you know? He looked good to me. I liked him. Mainly, he was scared as me, which I found real appealing."

On another occasion, Diane remembered that Woody Allen "looked like a little mole the first time I met him . . . It was him looking like a little mole that I was afraid of. And I thought surely I would be too tall for him."

Woody admits that he, too, was nervous about his audition with Keaton. "I was scared because—first of all, I had never acted in my life. I was strictly a night-club comic. And then, when we called her back we were worried that she'd be too tall, you know, and we didn't want the joke of the play to be that I was in love with—uh, you know—a super-looking woman.

"And so we got onstage together, and *both* of us were nervous. I felt, 'Oh, this is a real actress, she was in *Hair*, and I'm just going to waste her time' . . . and we measured back to back, and it was like being in the third grade."

When they measured back to back, Diane was a bit taller. Obviously, Woody and Joe Hardy didn't think it was an insurmountable problem because Diane got the part. They were both astonished at the way the other one dressed. "You never see him dressed up," Diane said, shortly after *Play It Again, Sam* began rehearsals. "He wears old, dirty tennis shoes, sweater and pants. I understand he wrote this show with the thought that he'd never have to change from his normal outfit."

For his part, Woody Allen had simply never seen a girl who dressed the way Diane did.

"She'd come in every day with an absolutely spectacularly imaginative combination of clothes. They were just great . . . She would come in with, you know, a football jersey and a skirt . . . and combat boots and, you know, oven mittens."

* * * * * *

While Woody had been making *Take the Money and Run*, his marriage to Louise Lasser had begun to come apart, a fact that probably bears some relation to the final version of *Play It Again, Sam*: a play about a man whose wife had just left him.

Allen Felix (Woody Allen) is a critic for a highbrow film quarterly. When his wife leaves him because he doesn't make her laugh enough (*"Insufficient laughter. When did that become grounds for divorce?"*), he sinks into a near-catatonic state in which he doesn't even bother to heat up his TV dinners. He just sucks them frozen.

Reality recedes—he's not sorry to see it go—and soon Allen is getting advice on how to make his love life something other than non-existent from none other than his boyhood idol, Humphrey Bogart.

Aiding Bogie's efforts back in the real world are Allen's best friend and his wife, Dick and Linda Christie, played by Tony Roberts and Diane, who introduce him to one girl after another, hoping that one of them will turn out to be Ms. Right.

Poor Allen, however, is so uptight about women at this point that he manages to screw things up with each and every sweet young thing that crosses—or is placed in—his path. The only woman he feels really comfortable with is Linda, who is drawn to Allen because he looks at her and listens to her and isn't always on the phone discussing business like her husband.

As the saying goes, one thing leads to another. Dick has to go to Cleveland on business. Allen and Linda plan to have dinner together at his place. They're not really surprised when they wake up the next morning in bed together.

Linda goes out to restock the larder for breakfast. While she's gone, who should turn up but Dick, home early from Cleveland and frantic that Linda is not at their apartment. Shortly after Dick arrives, Linda returns, domestically laden with groceries. This is the situation which allows Allen to deliver the speech he's been waiting to make all his life: the one Bogie gives in the penultimate scene of *Casablanca* when he relinquishes Ingrid Bergman forever.

Woody Allen described *Play It Again, Sam* as "an autobiographical story about a highly neurotic lover, an accumulation of themes that interest me: sex, adultery, extreme neuroses in romance, insecurity. It's strictly a comedy. There's nothing remotely non-comic about it."

He describes his method of playwriting as "reckless". When writing for the theatre, Woody says his attitude is: "To hell with it. I'll write the scene for twelve elephants. If it works, I've got an hysterical coup. If not, I'll cut it out of town.

"I've collaborated with other writers on a show or have been part of a team of six or more, sometimes simply in order to get the job, but the wonderful thing about a play is that you control your own material. You can do whatever you want."

One of the things Woody Allen does best is parody the serious works of others. A week before *Play It Again, Sam* opened on Broadway, Woody took a shot at reviewers, especially the ponderous, academic type. In the *New York Times*, Woody wrote a "review" of his upcoming theatrical effort:

"Play It Again, Sam *is a droll spoof aimed more at heart than the head, a puckish satire of contemporary mores based on the conquering of chapped lips by two British scientists in 1860. In his engaging way, Mr. Allen has given us not so much a play as three acts with a beginning, middle and end that build to a climax in the theatre.*

"Starting with a searing denunciation of Icelandic whaling techniques, the authors goes on to ask the question: Is anti-Semitism directed only at Jews? He plays with our emotions, exploring modern despair, death, loneliness and perversion, all with great warmth. He never condemns. He chooses instead to stand erect and whine.

"The action takes place in 1941 at a spelling bee in the Reichstag and later shifts its locale to between the toes of a giant named Grokon. (Students of Aramaic mythology will recognize Grokon as the procurer of the Golden Fleece and winner of the award for best dressed mythological giant two years running.)

"A lovable old character named Gramps—or Cramps (played by Mr. Allen, who can do more with the raising of an eyebrow than anyone in the theatre. Particularly if it is not his eyebrow) wanders in and out of the story, commenting wryly on the action and distributing hot rivets.

"By the end of Act I, the author's main contention is made clear: that capital punishment would be more effective as a preventive measure if it were administered prior to the crime.

"This notion is reworked in Act II where we are introduced to the Tristan motif as the theme suddenly shifts from man's inhumanity to man to, Are saddle shoes acceptable with a blue suit? These intellectualizations are played against one another contrapuntally with some extremely clever dialogue and a very wry remark I won't spoil by quoting, about suffocating to death in a locked closet.

"Act III concerns itself mainly with tying up the loose ends and pinpointing the responsibility for the overweight problem on the Pope who allegedly stood by and did nothing while a great many people ordered. There is a nude scene followed by a ballet depicting the stuffing of a flounder with crabmeat and, when the final curtain falls... we are left wondering: Is there a purpose to life, or do we just sit here or what? The title Play It Again, Sam *is taken cleverly from a passage in the Old Testament and is quoted in the playbill: "Anς' the prophet saith, play it again, Sam. And Sam did play it again and there was rejoicing and they made a covenant and got boils."*

During the period just after he had written *Play It Again, Sam*, Woody Allen still wasn't certain he wanted to star in it. There were so many other projects he was planning that the time factor had become a crucial consideration. "If I'm in *Play It Again, Sam*, I'm on Broadway for a year," Woody said to himself, trying to set the most productive priorities for himself. "If I'm on Broadway for a year, I would not be able to be in a movie or in nightclubs outside of New York. But in the time I would be in the play, I could write another play—and a movie. I would rather be in the play and not direct it, or direct it and not be in it . . . or not direct it and not be in it???"

The moment inexorably arrived when Woody had to make up his mind, and finally he chose to appear on stage in *Play It Again, Sam*. There were two reasons for deciding to go ahead and tie himself up for at least a year: he couldn't resist having his days free to write nor could he resist the part he'd written for himself in *Sam*. It was just too good to pass up.

The world of the theatre, however, was another matter. In

spite of his eagerness to write for Broadway, he had his doubts about it. "I find the theatre in the main very boring. It's a ponderous medium where everything is talk."

In spite of the fact that he had written *Play It Again, Sam* for himself, Woody was nervous about his decision to play the part of abandoned husband and unsuccessful womanizer Allen Felix on a New York stage. This would be far different from performing his own routines in a nightclub where he didn't have to worry about responding to other actors.

It would also be different from filming a movie in which you could shoot a scene over and over until you were satisfied with it.

Woody Allen knows he is not an actor in the way that Richard Burton or Rod Steiger or Alec Guinness is an actor. "I can act realistically within a certain narrow range," Woody says. "It's like Hope working with Crosby—Hope gives the correct response; it's not acting in the sense that Marlon Brando acts."

Even after rehearsals were underway, Woody continued to worry about his ability to give a good performance. At one point, he said to director Joe Hardy, "If I were the actor up there and I were the author out here, I'd come up behind you and say, 'What do you have that clown in this play for? Get him out. He's ruining my work."

Hardy saw that one of his jobs as director would be to get Woody "to be enlarged as an entity onstage." Slowly, Woody began to enjoy the process of working with the other actors.

Two days before *Sam* opened in New York, Harlene again filed suit against Woody, this time for $2 million. The first Mrs. Woody Allen claimed defamation and breach of a separation agreement. Also named in Harlene's lawsuit were NBC, Hackenbush Productions, Stage C Productions and Roncom Productions.

Her previous $1 million suit, filed early in 1967, had not yet come to trial. In it she claimed that Woody's jokes about her held her up to ridicule and public scorn. Both lawsuits were eventually settled out of court for an undisclosed amount and, presumably, Woody's promise to eliminate the ex-wife jokes from his repertoire.

Finally, *Play It Again, Sam* opened on Broadway at the Broadhurst Theatre. Minutes before the curtain rose on Act I,

Woody and Tony Roberts stopped by Diane Keaton's dressing room.

"Don't worry about your hands," they told her. "You'll be all right."

"What about my hands?" Diane asked. This was the first she'd heard about her hands being a problem.

"Just don't think about them," Tony said.

"You'll be all right," Woody assured her.

Diane spent opening night maddeningly aware of her hands.

* * * * * *

When *Don't Drink the Water* had opened in 1967, Woody had slipped away from the theatre on opening night before the first act curtain. (Later, however, he saw the play from beginning to end more than 100 times.) Obviously, an early departure did not seem a feasible course of action on the opening night of his second play: he was one of the actors this time as well as playwright. But Woody still managed to get away as soon as he could. He did not join the crowd at Sardi's to wait for reviews.

After a quiet supper with a few friends, he visited Louise. Even though no formal announcements had been made, Woody and Louise had been living apart for several months. They continued, however, to be friends. Woody had no idea what the reviews were like until the next morning. (The out-of-town critics in both Washington and Boston during the tryout period had been mostly enthusiastic.)

The news was mostly good. Nearly everybody loved *Play It Again, Sam* although the usual critical reservations were expressed. In the *New York Times*, Clive Barnes said that with his new play, Woody Allen "comes within stroking distance of real success, and his benignly frustrated presence is not only a joy forever, but together with his jokes and Joseph Hardy's quick-fire, slowburn staging, makes a slender but hilarious evening."

After describing *Sam's* plot twists, Barnes gets to the bad news: "Now for the sour cream. The play is so nearly so very good, that you wish Mr. Allen had aimed a little more accurately for a serious comedy of manners rather than just a situation farce. For not only are Mr. Allen's jokes—with their follow-ups, asides and twists—audaciously brilliant (only Neil Simon and Elaine May can equal him in this season's theatre), but he has a great sense of character. He is far from just being a gagman, but a theatrical talent that could, should and probably will do better....

"Mr. Allen has the heart of a comedian and the tongue of a comic, and it is no bad combination. He makes *Play It Again, Sam* into a cheerful virtuoso romp and, of course, he is joyous. But when you play it next time, Woody, how about transposing it into a slightly sadder key? It is only a suggestion—not that you should need one for the next year or so."

Barnes' prediction was correct. *Play It Again, Sam* had a run on Broadway of nearly a year. And Woody eventually took Barnes' advice and transposed his usual themes into a sadder key, although that did not occur until 1977's *Annie Hall*.

* * * * * *

A few months after *Play It Again, Sam* opened, Woody wrote a brief essay for *Life Magazine* explaining the origins of his passionate admiration of Humphrey Bogart.

"The first Humphrey Bogart movie I saw was The Maltese Falcon. *I was 10 years old and I identified immediately with Peter Lorre. The impulse to be a sniveling, effeminate, greasy little weasel appealed to me enormously and, setting my sights on a life of mealymouthed degradation and crime, I rapidly achieved a reputation that caused neighborhood parents to appear at my doorstep carrying torches, a large rope and bags of quicklime. This idolization of Lorre lasted until puberty, my sex glands suddenly making their debut like a Boston socialite and my interests turning rapidly from the sinister to the romantic. Now it was women—how to find, love them, leave them, and then go dig up fresh stock."*

After describing a particularly demeaning episode with the haughty Thelma Middleharnis, *"who though only 15 years old was endowed with sufficient physical attributes to melt the vault door at Chase Manhattan,"* Woody drowns his sorrows with an Orange Julius. Little does the crushed school-

boy realize that he is about to keep an appointment with
destiny.

*"Then I hit the flicks, as we called it, choosing a Bogart
double feature at a squalid return house, in the hopes of getting mugged and put out of my misery. This time, when* The
Maltese Falcon *came on I didn't identify with Peter Lorre.
My heart went directly to the master and I was hooked for
life.*

*"When Bogart, in love with Mary Astor as he was, turned
her in to the cops and calmly said, "I hope they don't hang
you by that precious neck, sweetheart," I drooled with an en-
vious worshipful drool that tapped the dregs of my salivary
glands. Why couldn't I have that same attitude when Thelma
Middleharnis gave me my walking papers?*

"All right, Thelma—you're taking the fall."

"No—darling—"

*"'Sorry, baby. If you get out of Tehachapi I'll be waiting
for you, and if you burn I'll come to the funeral.'*

*"I was talking aloud now and even the infamous clientele
of the Times Square movie house was getting up and moving
away from me. What I would have given at that moment to
send Thelma up—even if I had to frame her. I walked out of
that double feature a changed man...*

*"It wasn't long before I was walking like Bogart, talking
like Bogart, curling my lip and saying, 'No thanks, sweetheart. Oh, you're good. You're really good. Play it again,
Sam.' (I know he never actually said 'Play It Again, Sam' but
I said it enough for both of us.)"*

It works—after a fashion—until Woody meets Lou Ann
Monad, *"a hippie girl whose shape in a black leotard caused
my eyeballs to revolve like the fruit in a one-armed bandit."*
Woody and Lou Ann are inseparable for several months. Just
as Woody is about to ask Lou Ann to marry him, she leaves
him for the drummer in a rock group known as *The
Concluding Unscientific Postcript.* Clearly, it is time to fall
back on the unassailable strength and wisdom of Humphrey
Bogart.

*"I curled my upper lip and told her that she was a dame
and weak and quoted a passage of hard-line Bogey from* Key
Largo. *When that didn't work, I resorted to an emotional
plea culled from the high points of* Casablanca. *Then I tried*

something from The Big Sleep *and then* Sahara. *(Fortunately, what Bogart said about his tank in* Sahara *could also be applied to Lou Ann.) When it still left her unmoved, I fell back on* The Petrified Forest *and then* Sabrina. *Panicky now, I switched to a grubby Fred. C. Dobbs in* The Treasure of Sierra Madre *and asserted myself with the same petty ego he used on Tim Holt, to no avail. She laughed derisively, and moments later I found myself clicking two steel balls together and begging her not to leave me as I muttered something about the strawberries. I was given the gate.*

"Here was I, curled lip, five o'clock shadow, sibilant 's' and broken heart once again. I wrote Play It Again, Sam *to honor Bogart for at least giving me a few months of smooth sailing, and also to get even with a certain girl (or a particular sex that gives me trouble, to tell the truth).*

"While in rehearsal I happened to see The Maltese Falcon *again. I loved it just as much as ever, but I have come to one conclusion. The only safe thing is to identify with the actual falcon itself. After all, it's the stuff dreams are made on."*

* * * * * *

During the day, Woody continued to write. By now, nearly enough short pieces had appeared in *The New Yorker* to collect into a book. And he was putting together sketches for a new movie. Regularly, Woody was asked by various Broadway producers to tune-up their ailing shows. Just as regularly, Woody refused. "The only plays I want to doctor are my own plays," he said.

The chief drain on Woody's time that summer was an upcoming television comedy special for CBS, slated for airing in September. Woody had invited the Rev. Billy Graham, a favorite of then President Richard Nixon to appear with him. Graham, like William F. Buckley on Woody's last television special, was sure to provide maximum comic contrast, both visually and philosophically, to Woody himself.

He asked Graham to appear "because I'm an agnostic, he's a devout religious man, and we both have divergent views. What I'll do with Graham is just sit and talk. Naturally, I'll try and make it an exciting, amusing spot. I don't want to get into a boring, heavy religious discussion. I'll let the conversation go where it goes. The juxtaposition of the two of us is amusing to begin with."

Woody described himself as "an agnostic on the verge of becoming an atheist" but admitted that it was possible he was harboring a subconscious wish to be converted as evidenced by his choosing Billy Graham as a guest on his comedy hour. "Frankly, I'd loved to be converted. But that's not why I picked Graham. I wanted him on my show because he's an intelligent, liberal clergyman and I thought he'd offer an excellent contrast to me. My aim is for the session to be amusing."

Woody is a master of the titillating hype that is sure to increase the size of the audience. Several days before the show was scheduled for airing, Woody said, in his usual deadpan manner, that if Graham "struck a nerve" he just might be converted on camera. "I'm open to it and I'd be glad to have a go at it with him. Sure, I'd love to be converted. Life, it seems to me, is much easier if you're a believer. You can always come up with the easy answers."

Also appearing on the show were Candice Bergen and the Fifth Dimension, but the evening was dominated by Woody Allen performing his own sketches and monologues. Especially good was Woody's Chaplinesque version of a silent movie. He plays a garbage man briefly involved with an heiress.

Clearly, however, it was Woody's middle-of-the-show "conversation" with Billy Graham that got the most media attention. Woody said that he was careful to warn Graham in the very beginning that he would not be getting the treatment he was used to as America's No. 1 evangelist.

"I warned him right up front," Woody said. "When he was in the make-up room, I told him what I'd say in the introduction. Then I told him that we would take questions from the audience and just go for the—you know, try and keep it amusing if we can, rather than get into long heavy subjects. He said, fine, all he wanted was approval of the spot after it was over. He wanted to look at it before we put it on the air and see if there's anything there that embarrassed him. And I said sure."

ALLEN: My next guest is a very charming and provocative gentleman. Whether you agree with his point of view or not on things, he's always interesting to talk to. I don't agree with him on a great many subjects. There are a few we do agree on. But he's certainly the best in the world at what he does: Mr. Billy Graham.

Graham seemed perfectly at ease when he walked onstage. The audience was warmly welcoming. Then Woody and Graham sat down in the two facing chairs at the center of the stage. Woody asked his first question, and for just a moment Graham looked puzzled. But, showman that he is, Graham recovered quickly.

ALLEN: Can I ask you what your favorite commandment is?

GRAHAM: Well, right now, with a lot of teenagers, it's to honor your father and mother.

ALLEN: That's my least favorite commandment . . . I'm saving up my money, as I get a little bit successful in show business and when I get a little older . . . I'm going to put my parents in a home.

"I didn't know what to ask him really," Woody said. "That question came to me earlier but most of the questions were spontaneous. You have to plan a few questions beforehand because you don't want to get out there with him and have nothing happen."

ALLEN: Mr. Graham, I read that you don't believe in premarital sex relations, is this true?

GRAHAM: It's not a matter of what I believe, it's what the Bible teaches. The Bible teaches that premarital sex relations are wrong.

ALLEN: To me that would be like driving a car—you know, like getting a driver's license without a learner's permit first.

"I had no idea what he would say to this at all," Woody said. "I got the feeling after meeting him that he was going to be very pleasant to work with because there were only two possibilities at hand. One, he doesn't believe what he says and he's in it for the money; or, he's sincere. No reason to think that he's not. Therefore, while I don't agree with him, I do find him a nice guy. Who's really very pleasant, affable, a good person. I was very pleasantly surprised, charmed by him and taken by his theatricality; it overwhelmed. me."

GRAHAM: Well, but you see most psychologists today, and most psychiatrists, I think, would agree with the Bible that there are very serious problems involved. God didn't say thou shalt not commit immorality before marriage in order to keep you from having a good time or having fun.

ALLEN: Yes, He did.

Aside from the fact that Woody's three-word answer to Graham is very funny, it also represented an attitude toward established religion that is very rare on television, a medium which believes it can survive by offending the least number of persons, races, occupational and ethnic groups. When Woody first wrote this show, he had included a joke that referred to his own disheveled appearance: *Last year I made the best-dressed list . . . in Poland.* CBS executives insisted the joke be cut. Apparently, Polish-Americans have more clout with the networks than God. Possibly, this is because Polish-Americans write irate letters whereas God is generally silent and often hard to interpret when He finally decides to speak up. Woody, however, insists that he did not concern himself with a possible censorship battle with the network when he taped the Graham interview.

"No, I never felt intimidated," Woody said. "All I was thinking was that I hope we get something that plays funny. I was interested in the thing being amusing. I didn't want to make it into a denunciation of religion. Not that I don't feel that way. I *do*, but I just felt the whole idea of the comedy show was to get ten minutes between Graham and myself. If, in addition to that, there could be something interesting, then that's extra."

GRAHAM: Mr. Allen, what is the worst sin you ever committed?

ALLEN: The worst sin I ever committed? I had impure thoughts about Art Linkletter.

Clearly, this interchange was a set-up and in no way spontaneous. Woody, however, stone-walled it and insisted that the joke was not rehearsed.

"No, no, that's just a thing that happened," Woody declared. "I wish I had some of those. I combed my files beforehand for jokes that might be used. But you try to prepare yourself for these things, you get a lot of jokes in your mind and you're so tense about how you can work one in that it never works out. The best thing is just to take them as they come. The chemistry is so good in these situations that the audience is ready to laugh at anything. It's a big mistake to prepare too much."

GRAHAM: Every sin is the same in God's sight. I mean, there is no such thing as a worst sin.

ALLEN: Oh, really?

GRAHAM: If you wanted to find out which sin was the greatest, I would choose ... if I were forced to choose, I would say idolotry. Breaking the first commandment: "Thou shalt have no other Gods before me."

ALLEN: You mean that one bothers you the most?

GRAHAM: No, that doesn't bother me. That bothers the Scriptures. It bothers God ... because all the way God was teaching Israel, all through the Old Testament, that there was one God, only one, that we're to serve and we're to worship.

ALLEN: That seems to you an egomaniacal position?

GRAHAM: On God's part?

ALLEN: On God's part.

GRAHAM: Oh, no, God is perfect.

ALLEN: Yeah. You know, it's funny, when I look in the mirror in the morning, it's hard for me to believe that.

It is one thing to hint that God is a kill-joy who won't tolerate sex before marriage. It is quite another to call God an egomaniac because of his well-known position in Judeo-Christian circles of not wanting to look down on earth and see a lot of false gods cluttering up the landscape. It was at this point that Woody realized that this terrific little segment he was doing with the Rev. Billy Graham might not ever be seen by a national audience.

"You know, you're not even allowed to mention God on a show," Woody observed. "It always gets bleeped out. I mean, if I say, 'Oh my God' on the Carson show, you'll see my lips move but you'll never hear it. I was worried about that. I was thinking it would either be cut or we'd get such an amount of adverse mail. I hoped that every time Graham got laughs or ingratiated himself with the audience, it would add to the warmth of the spot. I didn't want it to seem niggling or mean."

ALLEN: You could probably convert me because I'm a pushover. I mean, I have no convictions in any direction and if you make it appealing enough and you promise me some sort of afterlife with a white robe and wings, I could go for it.

GRAHAM: Well, I don't promise you a white robe and wings but I can promise you a very interesting, thrilling life.

ALLEN: One wing maybe?

GRAHAM: ... You've got something in store for you. You see, you've experienced some of these other things but you haven't experienced God yet, and that's the greatest of all experiences and I'd hate for you to miss it.

ALLEN: Oh, I hate to miss it, if it's there. The question ...

GRAHAM: But it's there.

ALLEN: The question is—is it there?

GRAHAM: You're coming to our meeting. You'll see.

ALLEN: Yeah, I am ... I know the meeting will be there but will God show up?

GRAHAM: I believe He will.

"I was thinking of the theatrics of it all the time," Woody said. "Once in a while I would think, gee, he's taking too much time. Or, I hope we're not being too dull here. Before the interview I didn't have that high an opinion of Graham. I thought he was a clergyman who was doing it either for a buck, like most of them do, or he was dedicated and misguided. But then I was very charmed by him and very taken by his sincerity and I think he has come to a lot of correct conclusions the wrong way, for the wrong reasons ... But I was very taken by him. I felt a small pang of guilt over once having had the thought—oh, gee, I'll be out there with Graham and it will be a chance to score points and be really contrary to him. But I didn't feel that way when I was there; I felt here's a very decent guy who is trying to make an amusing spot."

ALLEN: ... But you're dressed very conservatively.

GRAHAM: Well, that was because I was on a previous show earlier and that was how I had to dress on that particular show and I didn't have time to change before I came over here to the studio.

ALLEN: Do you think that I ...

GRAHAM: I would have liked to have worn a very loud coat for this occasion.

ALLEN: Yeah, something casual? Devil-may-care? If you'll excuse the expression.

GRAHAM: (pointedly looking at Woody's blue sport

jacket) You mean something wild—like a blue coat or something like that—rather wild.

ALLEN: Yes, something really crazy like a blue coat.

The audience loved it and burst into enthusiastic applause. "That's when I was happiest, oddly enough, when he scored," Woody declared. "I didn't want it to seem that the guy was humorless and I was the comic or wise guy. There were a couple of times when he tried to be amusing and the audience was laughing and I liked that . . . It could only enhance the spot and I thought that would take the curse off any real conflict we might have.

"This has to be an instinctive thing," Woody continued. "I didn't ask the questions I might have. I got a letter from a lady who said she wanted me to ask him why he has not repudiated the story about the Jews killing Christ since so many Jews had suffered for this for so many years. I could have asked him that but that would have moved the whole thing into a real heavy area, an area that's not at all amusing. I could see Dick Cavett asking him that—the Cavett interviews are witty but essentially informative. This one I wanted to be funny."

It *was* funny . . . it was also bright, lively, irreverent, impertinent, and gentle. And although Woody Allen stoutly declares that the only thing he's interested in is the laugh . . . still, his encounter with Billy Graham showed that it is possible to disagree on important and substantive human issues without hatred, bitterness, strife, name-calling or denigration of the position that is not one's own. Surely, an important point to make in a melting pot nation.

ALLEN: Thank you for coming here and doing this with me, and you're always a treat to talk to and I hope I haven't provoked you or alienated you in any way?

GRAHAM: Oh, no, no. I've enjoyed it very much and I hope that we can do a repeat sometime. We've had a marvelous audience here and some wonderful questions, and I've thoroughly enjoyed it, and I want to say, God bless you.

Several weeks after Woody's CBS comedy special, a massive national Moratorium was planned by various groups opposing the Vietnam war. Set for October 15th, leaders of the protest hoped that everyone except persons working in essential services would take the day off. If the country came to standstill, they reasoned, perhaps Nixon, Kissinger and the Pentagon would understand that the American people did not support their ill-advised militaristic adventure in South Vietnam.

Woody Allen agreed to participate in the Moratorium by not appearing in *Play It Again, Sam*. He said he would go to an anti-war rally instead. Producer David Merrick, however, would not cancel the October 15th performances (there was a matinee) because, according to Woody, "he doesn't think it's an effective protest."

Woody said that everyone connected with *Play It Again, Sam* was in favor of the Moratorium and approved Woody's gesture of not showing up that day. Woody noted that their absences would be a violation of their contracts with Merrick and said, "I'm in a better position to do that than they are."

"I think increasingly dramatic gestures are needed to convince the government that the country wants the killing to stop," he said. Woody also urged other actors to observe the Moratorium.

* * * * * *

In November, the movie version of Woody's first play, *Don't Drink the Water*, was released. Starring Jackie Gleason and Estelle Parsons in the roles that Lou Jacobi and Kay Medford had undertaken in the Broadway production, the movie was "opened up" and included the chase scene which ends in the American Embassy, thereby creating the comic rationale for all the ensuing action.

Dick Libertini as the priest and amateur musician was the only member of the Broadway cast to appear in the movie. Although Woody's agent, Charles Joffe, produced the movie for Avco Embassy, Woody was not directly involved, probably because he was not able to negotiate the kind of professional *carte blanche* that he wanted for himself.

* * * * * *

During the run of *Play It Again, Sam*, Woody Allen and Diane Keaton spent increasing amounts of time together, often in the company of Tony Roberts, Diane's husband in the play. "We'd hang around together, nothing big, have dinner," Woody says. "Tony and I couldn't stop laughing at Diane. It was nothing you could quote later; she couldn't tell a joke if her life depended on it. Tony tried to figure it out one time, what it is she does. He says she has this uncanny ability to project you back into an infantile atmosphere, and you are suddenly a little kid again. There is something utterly guileless about her. She's a natural.

"And I thought she was very charming to be around, and of course you always get the impulse with Diane to protect her. And she was so bright and quick. She's also a real easy laugher, which is very seductive, and we kind of drifted together is what happened," Woody added.

Even though Diane Keaton's career did not truly blossom until years later, Woody says he knew at the time that she would one day be a major actress. "It was inevitable," he said. "It was just apparent the minute I was acting with her in *Play It Again, Sam* that she was a major comic talent. And it was confirmed for me by people who would come to the show."

One night, for example, Jack Benny showed up. Backstage, after the performance, he told Woody, "That girl is going to be gigantic."

The role of Linda in *Play It Again, Sam* brilliantly utilizes several of Keaton's special traits: her lovable flakiness, her emotional vulnerability, her aura of self-effacement . . . all of which make men want to protect her. Women aren't threatened because most of them immediately identify with the woman that Keaton projects.

"I think it's something that she grew up with, and she probably learned at an infant's age that that kind of thing is very endearing to people," Woody says. "But it's not at all calculated. Tony Roberts used to feel that she was the type that would wake up in the morning and *immediately* start apologizing. She's one of those people who is forever putting herself down—and always coming through."

During the months they were hanging out together, Keaton and Tony Roberts began addressing Woody as "Max" in order to lessen the chances that he would be recognized—and confronted—by over-zealous fans. The nickname stuck. To Diane Keaton, Woody Allen has been "Max" ever since.

* * * * * *

Play It Again, Sam closed early in 1970. As the new decade began, Woody Allen was spending most of his time on the myriad details involved in making a movie, the one that would eventually become *Bananas*. Woody asked Louise Lasser, from whom he was now divorced, if she would appear in it with him. She accepted.

Louise had begun to achieve public recognition on her own via a commercial she'd done for a cold remedy. She played a solicitous wife named Mildred who ministers to her husband, devastated by a head cold, by providing him with various comforts including, of course, the sponsor's cold remedy.

He looks up gratefully and speaks to her through his clogged sinuses. "You're a good wife, Mildred."

"I know. I know," Louise says.

Louise was mystified at the way the spot caught on. "I certainly wasn't trying to be funny in the commercial," she said. "The strange part is that people remembered it even when it hadn't been on the air in years."

One day a man stopped her on the street. "I keep telling my wife that if she could only be like you we'd have a happier marriage," he said.

"In reality, I was the worst wife imaginable," Louise confessed. "Just ask Woody Allen."

Neither Woody nor Louise ever spoke publicly about the reasons they were divorced. When the news leaked out that Louise would have the major female role in Woody's second movie, there was talk that they had reconciled and would remarry. No one could believe that two people who had once been married could end up as friends.

"Woody's a very good husband—well, a very good second ex-husband—to have used me in the picture. You remember what he said about my cooking? That he realized I wasn't much of a chef when he found a bone in the chocolate pudding? It's true. I am very inept in the kitchen," Louise said.

On those rare occasions when Woody made a personal appearance, he continued to use some of the ex-wife jokes for which Harlene had sued him. They didn't bother Louise, however.

"As long as he makes clear that the things he says about his ex-wife are about his first ex-wife and not his second ex-wife, I'm not disturbed," she said. "I feel sure he'd never say those things about his *second* ex-wife."

When Woody was asked why he and Louise had divorced, he said they had done it "as a protest against the Vietnam war. Some people set themselves on fire. We got a divorce."

He described Louise's role in the new film: "It's the part of a charmingly neurotic, very predatory, very aggressive girl. I have great confidence in her as a talented comedienne . . . She's very easy to work with. Of course, she's known me rather well."

* * * * * *

Bananas, like *Take the Money and Run*, has the thinnest of plots. Fielding Mellish (Woody Allen) is a products tester in Manhattan and falls desperately in love with Nancy (Louise Lasser) who is a girl eager to participate in the revolution if she can just find out where they're holding it. Fielding can't measure up to her requirements for passion, truth and relevance so he takes off for an unnamed banana republic and joins a band of guerrillas in their mountain stronghold. He will show Nancy that he's just as relevant as anybody.

On this slim plot structure, Woody hangs his usual outrageous bits. The movie opens with Howard Cosell and the ABC *Wide World of Sports* crew covering the Assassination of the Week. The man targeted for this honor is the President of San Marcos. His assassination will climax a gala week that began with the sacking of the U.S. Embassy.

The timing is perfect, but of course it has to be: television is a very exact medium. El Presidente strides out of his palace to greet the crowd and, within seconds, is shot. Pandemonium erupts and Howard Cosell quickly moves through the near-hysterical throng toward the fallen dictator, all the while giving us a superb play-by-play.

Finally, Cosell reaches El Presidente, inelegantly sprawled

on the palace steps. He thrusts the microphone into his face, but it's too late. We have missed El Presidente's last words. He is quite dead.

Then the titles start to run and we're back in New York, watching Fielding as he reaches his decision: he will join the freedom fighters in San Marcos.

Howard Cosell's brief bit in *Bananas* was filmed in a day. Cosell flew to Puerto Rico in the morning, Woody spent just two hours getting the assassination segment on film, and then Cosell flew back to New York in the evening.

"I like to work fast and carelessly," Woody said. "This kind of comedy should look disjointed, not slick like a Ross Hunter picture or an Antonioni film—not that I think I could do that—but I prefer the rough look. If you look back at the films of the Marx Brothers and Chaplin they are all sort of slapdash. I saw *The Gold Rush* just the other day. And, although the important things in it were exquisitely directed, the general feeling is so rough-hewn."

Woody said that he considered Howard Cosell "a young Bela Lugosi" and hoped he could use him again in another movie. "I want to make films that don't cost much and that express my form of humor. Fortunately, I work for a particularly enlightened company (United Artists) and they give me complete freedom," Woody said.

In *Bananas*, Woody paid homage to Swedish director Ingmar Bergman and to the great Russian filmmaker, Sergei Eisenstein. In the scene derived from Bergman, two groups of black-robed and hooded monks are carrying crosses on a deserted Wall Street. There is only one parking place and soon the two groups of monks are battling over it.

The reference to Eisenstein is just a brief flash: a baby buggy is seen bouncing down the stairs on some sort of public plaza. This moment, of course, refers to the famous scene in *Potemkin* when a baby carriage hurtling down the stairs is meant to symbolize the chaos of social disorder and revolution.

It is curious, however, that while Woody Allen gives lip service to the greatness of directors like Bergman and Eisenstein, his references to their work in his own movies invariably trivialize and degrade the work of these monumental filmic artists.

Among the more hilarious takes in *Bananas* is the look on Fielding's face when he reads a headline that says "New York Rifle Council Declares Death a Good Thing" and the moment when Fielding hears harp music (Does Death beckon?), then discovers the music is easily explained: there's a man playing a harp in his closet.

At one point, a very substantial black woman takes the stand and must give her name to the judge, the jury and the assembled spectators in the courtroom. She raises her right hand, takes the oath and gives us her name. "I am J. Edgar Hoover," she declares.

"I didn't have the joke until the woman came in for casting," Woody said. "She looked like Hoover, so I wrote it in."

Near the end of the movie, the freedom frighters have been successful and General Emilio M. Vargas (Carlos Montalban), with whom Fielding has been playing guerrilla in the mountains, is named President of San Marcos by popular acclaim. The honor is more than he can handle. In an ebullient speech and for reasons not immediately discernible, he declares Swedish to be the national language.

The movie ends with Howard Cosell narrating the on-camera consummation of a marriage in the bridal suite of the Royal Manhattan Hotel. Yes, there is an instant replay.

* * * * * *

As a film maker, Woody was learning on the job. "I wanted to make this a pretty picture as well as a funny one," he said. Most of the San Marcos exteriors were shot in Puerto Rico, including the streets, plazas and docks of Old San Juan.

During one particularly gruelling week, Woody and the crew left their hotel in San Juan at 4 a.m. for a ninety-minute drive to a Cerra Gordo location. Woody wanted everything set up so they could get just the right light for a scene set at dawn.

In spite of this attention to technical details and his desire to make a "pretty" picture, Woody Allen was well aware that his movies were not just comedies, but "comedian's pictures." He explained the difference.

"A comedian's picture is about the comedian. It is highly

dependent on the personality of the comedian and not a story to be acted. If you have two stiffs doing Laurel and Hardy, it wouldn't be Laurel and Hardy."

Woody said that he makes a point of looking at the classic comedies of the 1930's again and again, especially those of the Marx Brothers, W.C. Fields and Charlie Chaplin. "It's too late not to be influenced by them," he said. He doesn't go to see contemporary comedies for the same essential reason: he doesn't *want* to be influenced by them. "They cause me anxiety."

Besides, for Woody, sometimes a film that wasn't intended to be a comedy serves that function for him anyway. *The Oscar* is a case in point. It is Woody Allen's favorite terrible movie, "Conceivably the worst movie ever made. It's so rich in esthetic incorrectness. There is an unself-conscious badness about it."

He "enjoyed" *The Oscar* so much that he once borrowed a print of it and invited several sets of friends over to his house to see it.

Aside from anomolies like *The Oscar*, Woody prefers serious movies. "They're so clearly what not to do in comedy. They're so antithetical to laughter." He is constantly drawn to the work of Ingmar Bergman and the Spanish director Bunuel. Even in 1971, Woody toyed with the idea of making a film with a theme as serious as one of Bergman's. "I lack his intellect, technique and talent," Woody said, "but apart from that . . . If I directed *Hamlet* a scene that was touching and profound would be totally vacuous."

Since the early 1970's, Woody has sent up these trial balloons. He suggests in an interview the possibility of a serious Woody Allen film, then quickly scoffs at his own idea. When it comes to comedy, however, Woody seems very sure of himself. "Nobody can make my films better than I can," he says.

"I cast quickly. I see actors only for a minute. Not that much is required. What interests me is the look. Jokes have got to be visual. The trick in a comedian's film is to have a thin story to hang the comedy sequences on. And to tell it step by step in very extravagant terms. Mickey Rose and I write the script, and then 50 per cent of the movie is improvised.

"Laughs are not subordinate to color or camera movement," Woody said. "I have been so tempted to put a long lens on the camera, to lay down the dolly tracks, but it would have hurt the laughs. You move only to kill boredom."

Getting the laughs is so important to Woody that it astonishes him when obscure political or philosophical interpretations are made of a work that he views as entertainment, pure and simple. Those viewers and critics with a bent for this type of analysis had a field day with *Bananas*, whose theme was apparently revolution.

"I've always tried not to be a topical satirist because it dates so quickly. You can get cheap laughs making Nixon jokes and it seems like you're saying something, too, but five years later the stuff will be dead as can be. I like a broader kind of humor, one that's less calculated. *Bananas* revolves around a good theme—revolution—and that was luck. When I was in Europe, the obsession of the reporters was political. They couldn't care less if there were laughs in the picture. They wanted to know, 'What were the politics of *Bananas?*' and 'How do you feel about revolution?' They thought the greatest impact in the picture came when the hoods attacked a woman in the subway. To them, that personified America, but they missed the whole comic point.

"*Bananas* was a fast movie but I want to make one even faster, using the same technique I see in S.J. Perelman's writing—making a joke on the way to a joke with a joke in the background.

"I hate politics. Political thinking throughout history has never worked. As long as it's a question of is it going to be Democrat or Republican, Communist or whatever, as long as people delude themselves into thinking if they can solve those issues they'd be happy, nothing's going to happen. I think that if there were only two people in the world and they were identical twins, one would find something wrong with the other somehow."

One of the political issues Woody had to deal with before *Bananas* was released was the question of its rating. The Motion Picture Association had at first given *Bananas* an "R" rating. The bottom line difference between "R" and the far more acceptable "GP" can run into hundreds of thousands of dollars. The major studios frequently use considerable pressure to have an "R" changed to a "GP". Woody used a different tactic: "We were begging."

Woody considers the rating system a deterrent to the entire movie industry. "Do you know that there are 1,000 theaters in this country that won't take an R-rated movie? The sufferers are the public. Once a picture is rated, the theaters should show it and let the public decide whether or not it wants to see it."

In the case of *Bananas*, a great many people wanted to see it in spite of the fact that, according to Woody, the movie was "never aimed in a big, mass way. The fact that it is doing business in a big way only proves how starved everyone is for film comedies.

"I'm the only one making the traditional American comedy complete with sight gags and everything," Woody said. "People do serious comedies, like *Little Murders*. There is the talk comedy which is what Jack Lemmon does like the ones written by Neil Simon; but there are no comedies in which chase sequences and sight gags are indigenous."

But of course the key ingredient in a Woody Allen film is neither wild chase scenes nor improbable sight gags. What makes Woody's movies work is Woody's own comic sensibility which he trusts without question. He usually shows a rough cut of a just-completed movie to a small audience. "I screen it under the worst possible conditions—very astringently," Woody says.

He pays close attention to where the laughs come. Gathering this information is, after all, the purpose of the screening. But in the final analysis, Woody follows his own comic judgment. Even though one joke in *Bananas* wasn't as successful in previews as he'd hoped, he refused to cut it. This was the scene in which someone is tortured by being forced to listen to a continual playing of a recording of *Naughty Marietta*. A similar scene occurred in *Take the Money and Run* when Virgil-Woody runs afoul of a Southern prison guard and is locked into a sweltering solitary confinement cell with a life insurance salesman.

On the basis of a mere two movies—hardly an oeuvre—discerning and imaginative Woody Allen buffs had plucked out a noticeable and mysterious symbol: in both *Take the Money and Run* and *Bananas*, the parents of the Woody-Virgil-Fielding protagonist are masked. Their faces are hidden from view by a Groucho Marx disguise in *Take the Money and Run* and by surgical masks—they're both doctors—in *Bananas*.

When this recurrent motif was pointed out to him, Woody said, "I'm not sure what that represents. Perhaps something deep in my subconscious... I wonder if it might have re-occured spontaneously in the next movie."

Later, after he'd had some time to think about it, Woody explained his symbols: "My parents deserve to be masked."

Another theme was food. There was that steak cooked in its cellophane wrapping in *Take the Money and Run*. In that same movie, Virgil has in his wallet a carefully folded piece of bologna that he divides up with his wife and son when they're on the lam. Later, when Louise visits him in prison, she brings Virgil something to eat: a hard-boiled egg which she slowly pushes through the grating in the visiting room. In *Bananas*, the band of mountain guerrillas stop in a small roadside restaurant and order 1,000 grilled cheese sandwiches.

"I think food is funny," Woody explains. "Like sex. Food and sex are always good for a laugh."

* * * * * *

Bananas was released in April, 1971, and a month later Woody published another of his tongue-in-cheek critical essays in the *New York Times*. This latest effort was sort of on the topic: *How To Be a Film Critic*. Sort of. Woody managed to sound as if he had been trapped at a long dinner party between Robert Brustein and Susan Sontag:

"Film or cinema or even 'movies', although 'movies' connotes a picture or motion picture or form of cinema as opposed to, say, film or a photoplay which indicates a picture or pictures on film or cinema on film which characteristically implies a subjective movie consciousness or filmic response, is essentially a visual medium as differentiated from, say, radio which is almost totally aural. (Turn off the radio and see how hard it is to hold your interest.)

"Definitions, incidentally, here are important, as they tend to objectify or conceptualize without identifying precisely the mode of direct apprehension of the viewer or reader or subject, as it were, and provide guidelines for he or she to eventually doze off. Obviously, film is a young art and as such is not truly an art but an art within an art employing the devices of mass communication in a linear, non-modal, anti- or non-diversified, creative otherness which we will call den-

sity. If a picture is dense, it has density. This concept was first borrowed from the French and then before it could be returned to them was misplaced by the prop department.

"We go to the movies because a picture is playing there. Griffith knew that and said it repeatedly but always to his cat rather than the studio heads. Truffaut, of course, always refers to his films as movies and his movies as films. He also refers to himself as Godard, because Truffaut, he feels, has a pseudo-arty, non-proletarian quality while Godard is much easier to spell.

"The true nature of film is that it is not literature. It is not painting, in fact it is not even film. That's the part that confuses most people. The key word here, by the way, is "plastic". Soon everything will be made out of plastic and what will happen to the small tradesman who enjoys working with wood? It will be tough on him. Very tough. Kurosawa deals with that exact problem in Itzemetzu *(loosely translated,* The Shepherd's Ointment*) and comes to grips with it or something comes to grips with him. The point is, he was found last week on the floor unconscious.*

"What then is the function of the critic? Precisely to interpret the audio-visual electronic image and fragmentize individual coercive response against a background of selective subjectivity. He can do this either standing up or sitting and some of the better ones spend a lot of time in hotel rooms with women they're not married to. Also to alert the public to new dimensions in art and of course, whenever possible, to point out where the fire exits are. This is particularly true in comedy which is, in general, more audio-visual oriented in a totally non-supportive McLuhanian juxtaposition of related factors than, say, my mother is. Laughter, remaining subconscious in its manifest realm (or as Freud put it, when it comes out of the mouth) often works best after something funny has happened. This is why the death of a friend almost never gets a chuckle but a funny hat does."

This outrageously effective spoof of critical jargon continues for several more paragraphs. This parody is especially funny when you remember that Woody made his comic character in *Play It Again, Sam* a critic on a highbrow film quarterly. In other words, a man would probably write in all seriousness what Woody wrote in jest.

* * * * * *

As soon as the filming and editing of *Bananas* was completed, Woody was back at work on two nearly simultaneous movie projects. He was writing a screen version of *Play It Again, Sam* plus a movie based on David Reuben's best-selling potboiler *Everything You Always Wanted to Know about Sex but Were Afraid to Ask*. And, of course, Woody continued writing for *The New Yorker*. Woody Allen maintained a work schedule that one U.S. newsweekly described as "demonic".

"Woody's life is his work," Diane Keaton said. "He is just not a relaxer. I can't imagine him lounging around the pool in the sunshine in that white skin."

"I have to work every day," Woody admitted. "Otherwise I hear voices nagging me on and on."

Woody had decided not to direct himself in the movie version of *Play It Again, Sam*. Instead, he asked Broadway and Hollywood veteran Herbert Ross to sit in the director's chair. Ross, also a Brooklyn native, moved to Miami Beach with his family when he was 11 years old and hated it. Still, he got his first job there working in the Coral Gables Swim Show.

When Ross was 15, he took $100 he had saved and came back to New York—Manhattan, not Brooklyn—where he faked his age, won a scholarship to study with Herbert Berghof, played Shakespeare on the road and began dancing. Soon, Ross moved into choreography. The Broadway musical was his specialty but he also served a tour of duty as resident choreographer for the American Ballet Theatre. In 1959, Ross married ballerina Nora Kay.

The move to Hollywood was inevitable. He choreographed *Funny Girl*. Barbra Streisand was so impressed with his work that she asked Ross to direct her in a non-musical, *The Owl and The Pussycat*. Since then, Ross has worked as a straight film director rather than as choreographer for musicals.

At first, Ross was curious why Woody didn't want to direct himself as he had done in *Take the Money and Run* and *Bananas*. Then Ross realized that Woody "wanted it to be different as a film, to have more dimensions."

As a play, *Sam* had been set in New York, but Woody

wanted to "open up" the movie and decided to set it in his second favorite American city: San Francisco. It was a good decision. The San Francisco exteriors act as a humanizing backdrop to Allen Felix's (Woody Allen) neurotic ways of relating to life and to women. Allen's limitations do not seem either boring or self-indulgent as well they might have if, following the stage version, the movie had taken place primarily in Allen's New York apartment.

Among the San Francisco locations used were the bandshell in Golden Gate Park, the Museum of Art, the Trident Restaurant on the bay, Cunio's Italian Bakery, Ray's Laundromat, the Spaghetti Factory cabaret and a couple of splendid hillside apartments. The interiors were shot at Paramount's Hollywood studios.

By the time they began filming *Play It Again, Sam*, Diane Keaton and Woody Allen had been living together for several months in the duplex that Woody had bought in 1969 on Fifth Avenue in the Seventies.

* * * * * *

ALVY: You're not gonna give up your own apartment, are you?

ANNIE: Of course, because I'm moving in with you.

ALVY: But you've got a nice apartment.

ANNIE: I have a tiny apartment . . . and it's got bad plumbing and bugs.

ALVY: All right, granted it has bad plumbing and bugs, but you say that as if it's a negative thing. You know bugs . . . entymology is a rapidly growing field.

ANNIE: You don't want me to live with you.

ALVY: I mean we live together, we sleep together, we eat together—Jesus—you don't want it to be like we're married, do you?

ANNIE: How is it any different?

ALVY: It's different 'cause you keep your own apartment.

ANNIE: That little apartment is $400 a month, Alvy!

ALVY: That place is $400 a month?

ANNIE: Yes, it is.

ALVY: But it's got bad plumbing and bugs.

From a scene in *Annie Hall*

* * * * * *

Woody had felt forced to leave the brownstone duplex he had shared with Louise Lasser because it was too accessible to the public. Woody's teen-age fans, especially, would sit on the front stoop from morning 'til night waiting for him to leave the house or arrive back home. They would throw pebbles at the windows in hopes of getting Woody's attention. They would ring the doorbell. Ignoring the well-publicized fact that Woody writes all his own material, they would leave scripts, plays and comedy routines for him to read.

In contrast, the Fifth Avenue apartment is many floors up from street level, overlooking Central Park. Its windows are beyond the reach of New York's champion pebble throwers. Two doormen in the lobby shoo fans away. Clearly, a much better set-up for a man who likes his privacy as much as Woody Allen does.

The 11-room duplex had originally been two apartments. Woody bought both units and had them rebuilt into a single, spacious home. When Diane moved in early in 1971, the apartment was still largely unfurnished and Diane helped Woody decorate, choosing rugs, wing chairs, cannisters, china, books... everything in rich, dark colors that seem to be made for the apartment of a corporation lawyer rather than the abode of a comic genius. (Then, of course, one realizes that Woody could not have acquired the elegant apartment in the first place had he actually been as inept as the comic persona he has so carefully and brilliantly created.)

In 1969, Diane had a small part in *Lovers and Other Strangers*, a romantic comedy written by the husband and wife team of Renee Taylor and Joseph Bologna. She also played the self-effacing Kay, long-suffering wife to Al Pacino's Michael in *The Godfather*, a movie in which she was all but invisible. *Play It Again, Sam* was Diane's first substantial movie role, Woody having made her part considerably more extensive than the stage version when he wrote the screenplay.

And, of course, film is surely a much more effective medium for a quiet, understated actress like Diane Keaton. Film, via the close-up, can catch the fleeting expressions of vulnerability, amazement and gentleness that breeze across Keaton's face in subtle and complex relays. All this delicacy would be lost on stage, at least to anyone not sitting in the first five rows. Director Ross described Keaton as "a splendid actress, mature for her age."

Ross was also enthusiastic about Woody's deciding to shoot the film in San Francisco: "Making pictures in California is much easier and simpler than working on them in New York. Those studios out there have the best facilities, the best technicians in the world, and any American location you want is nearby (on the back lots.)

"In New York, there are headaches, permits, rival unions badgering a producer, small irritations like scouting for locations and people on the street interrupting shooting."

Ross had an even higher opinion of Woody Allen, describing him as "impeccable in his behavior" as well as "intelligent, cooperative, talented, patient, perfect and terrific."

"Woody was delightful to work with," Ross added, "unassuming, no cranky kicks. If he thought his story needed doctoring, he came to me, and together we worked out something that satisfied him. And me."

Jerry Lacy, the actor who played Bogart in the Broadway production, was retained for the movie production. "It's the best imitation of Bogart I've seen," Ross said. Indeed, it does sound like Bogie himself advising Woody Allen on how to handle women: "*I never met one who didn't understand a slap in the mouth or a slug from a .45.*"

This advice is, however, somewhat wasted on a man who not only douses himself with Canoe before a big date but drinks a healthy slug as well.

Everyone knows that only the things you figure out for yourself are truly effective . . .

* * * * * *

It is the morning after Allen and Linda have made love for the first (and as it happens, the last) time.

LINDA: What were you thinking about while we were doing it?

ALLEN: Willie Mays.

LINDA: Do you always think about baseball players when you're making love?

ALLEN: Keeps me going.
LINDA: Yeah . . . I couldn't figure out why you kept yel-
ling, 'Slide!'
ALLEN: I was fantastic.
LINDA: I think the Pepto-Bismol helped.

* * * * * *

Allen's experience with Linda forever frees him from the impossible standards of Humphrey Bogart, a man who never really existed, a man wholly created by the Hollywood dream factory. Allen "gives up" Linda to Tony in a conscious re-enactment of Bogart "giving up" Ingrid Bergman to Paul Henried with the speech that still stands as a great cinematic moment: compassion, generosity, honor and the destruction of Fascism were held to be more important than meeting one's own narrow needs.

In the renunciation of Linda and of his fantasy of impossible masculinity, Allen is freed to be himself. As Bogart is about to fade from his life forever, Allen says, *"You're tall and ugly and you made it. I'm short and ugly and I'll make it."*

Play It Again, Sam is different—and better—than Woody Allen's other movies, most probably because he did not direct. Woody still plays himself, of course, and there are still a few of those slapstick moments when Woody is unable to open a bathroom cabinet without the contents cascading over him to the floor. This last shtick was old when Fibber McGee and Molly were using it. Does such a lazy device, totally unmotivated, truly belong in a romantic comedy in the 1970's? For the most part, however, Ross keeps Woody's self-indulgence to a minimum and manages to get a straight-forward, disciplined performance from him.

Another reason that *Play It Again, Sam* has worn so much better than Woody's other movies is simply that it is more human. It tells a story that reverberates for most of us. How do we find someone to love? How do we deal with our inadequacies? How do we get those silly celluloid fantasies out of our heads? The movie also achieved what Woody had tried and failed to achieve in *Bananas*. Ross made *Sam* both pretty and funny.

Audiences agreed that *Play It Again, Sam* was a winner. Released in May, 1972, *Sam* had grossed $11 million by 1975.

* * * * * *

In the fall of 1971, before Woody and Diane left for San Francisco to begin shooting *Sam*, Woody had written and produced a comedy special for public television. Scheduled for airing on February 21, 1972, the program was a political satire aimed at the Nixon Administration.

In 1972, Richard Nixon and his henchmen were hard at work trying to guarantee themselves victory in the November election. Their methods, as has been documented in sworn testimony before numerous federal judges, included burglary, blackmail, extortion, myriad forms of deceit including so-called "dirty tricks" as well as the use of various federal agencies for purposes of intimidation.

The Nixon White House was especially annoyed by the programs they saw on public television. PBS (Public Broadcasting System) programs were frequently bright, lively and irreverent, qualities not appreciated by embryonic dictatorships. So the Nixon Administration sent PBS general manager Gerald Slater an easily understood message.

The messenger and hatchet man in Nixon's plan to emasculate all public forums where reasoned debate and political dissent might occur was Clay T. Whitehead, director of the White House Office of Telecommunications Policy. And sadly, in the U.S. of the 1970's, there were virtually no public forums that approached the impact of television. Even public television with a mere fraction of the networks' audiences could still claim hundreds of thousands of viewers across the country, most of whom were voters.

White delivered his message at a House Subcommittee meeting several weeks before *The Politics and Humor of Woody Allen* was due to be shown. Whitehead said that PBS had moved "too far" in the direction of network programming at the expense of local initiative. Then Whitehead said the Administration would not support long-term financing of public television "at this time."

The threat—and the deal they were willing to make— couldn't have been more clear. If PBS cuts out "liberal" programming and stops giving access to the public airways to Nixon's enemies, then money will be forthcoming and everybody can keep their jobs.

In one segment of Woody's show called "Men of Crisis", Woody plays Dr. Harvey Wallinger, a top Presidential adviser, known for his jet-setting and his penchant for squiring beautiful women. Any resemblance to former Secretary of State Henry Kissinger was not coincidental. Dr. Wallinger got his Ph.D. in needlepoint at Harvard. According to the script, Wallinger was born of German-Jewish extraction and was named after Rabbi Fats Gillespie, the Jazz Rabbi. His father, Dr. Herbert Wallinger, makes his living performing open-heart surgery by mail. His mother, the former Anna Cheswick, is a newspaper woman who had an affair with Mussolini until she discovered he was Italian. Wallinger's heroes are Aaron Burr and the Kaiser.

Elsewhere in the show, Woody said he "loathed" the Nixon Administration.

At first, PBS tried to accommodate the White House by offering its 219 member stations an alternative show, a one-hour satire called *Come to Florida Before It's Gone*, starring Myron Handelman. PBS director of public information Edward Morris said the network had decided to offer the option after Billy B. Oxley, a PBS program coordinator, warned that Woody's show might engender "problems of equal time, personal attack, the fairness doctrine and the subjective issue of taste."

"In considering these questions," Morris explained, "we decided to substitute another program in our scheduled service for February 21 and . . . prefeed the Allen show to the stations on February 15. The stations would then be in a position to preview it themselves in the light of the questions raised and make their own decision whether they wished to run it. They are free to do so if they want. Our feeling was that we did not want to place their licenses in jeopardy."

The last sentence in Morris' statement seems, on close examination, rather strange. Woody's show contained newsreel footage of Minnesota Senator Hubert Humphrey, Alabama governor George C. Wallace and President Richard Nixon, all of them announced presidential candidates. This meant that other presidential contenders had a right to equal time—

and nothing more. There is nothing in the FCC statutes that would allow a President to lift a broadcasting license because the station in question satirized him or his administration. Nor is there any provision for revoking a license because a station airs a program that many persons are likely to find in bad taste. And Woody cheerfully admitted his send-up of Henry Kissinger was "in bad taste, there's no question about it. Because I'm a master of bad taste and it's hard to do anything about the administration that wouldn't be in bad taste."

PBS general manager Slater insisted there was no connection between Whitehead's statement before the House subcommittee concerning the refusal of the Nixon Administration to support public television "at this time" and the PBS decision to drop Woody's show from the prime time schedule. "That has nothing to do with it," Slater said. "We have not been in touch with them (the White House). It's just that this is a biting satire that singles out only one candidate during a political year."

Woody's show had been produced by WNET (Channel 13), the PBS station in New York, with Woody's agent Charles Joffe serving as executive producer, a function he had also performed on *Take the Money and Run* and *Bananas*. WNET vice president and general manager Jay Iselin said in a carefully worded statement that he was planning to run the show on his station. New Yorkers, at least, would have a chance to see what all the fuss was about.

"It appears we've managed to produce a mouse that might scare the President," Iselin said, adding that his understanding of the difficulty was that the show chided President Nixon, thus giving him, as a declared presidential candidate, the right to equal time.

"If that's possible, it would be great," Iselin declared. "I have every intention of running the program if that's the only problem with it. And I hereby invite President Nixon to reply to it on our station if he wants to." He said that WNET lawyers had looked at the show after its completion and did not find any objectionable or potentially troublesome material. In spite of this clean bill of political health, WNET executive vice president Ward Chamberlin withdrew the program from PBS distribution so that the lawyers could look at it again. There would be no broadcast of the program until this second legal review was completed.

This was the first hint that the show would be completely withdrawn. Earlier in the day, PBS had said the show would be made available to those stations that wanted to go ahead and put it on the air.

All this took place on Friday, February 11, 1972. It would be interesting to check the White House phone bills for that week-end. Pressure was definitely applied, but without records it's difficult to know by whom to whom.

By Monday, however, a number of key persons in public television had developed new points of view. Iselin, for example, said that while he was still anxious to carry Woody's show, he now believed it would benefit from a new introduction and conclusion.

"It's a marvelously funny show," Iselin said, "but the intro and exit deal entirely with comedy as an art form. I would like to see Mr. Allen re-do those pieces with an intro on the problems and prospects of political satire. Our attorneys are still looking it over, but if equal time is the only problem, Channel 13 will go ahead with it and give the time to anyone who asks for it."

Other public television executives, however, saw equal time as an issue that would allow them to avoid the ire and possible retaliation of the White House and still manage to save face. They wouldn't save much, but no doubt felt a little was better than none at all.

James Day, president of the Educational Broadcasting Corporation of which WNET was part, said that *The Politics and Humor of Woody Allen* was being withdrawn from national distribution for further study because he was afraid the show was in violation of Section 315 of the Federal Communications Act. Section 315 was the equal time provision...

Which makes it all the more ironic that one of the guests on *Come to Florida Before It's Gone*, the show that replaced Woody's, was Pat Paulsen, a not-totally-serious but very official candidate for president. Paulsen qualified to be on the ballot in New Hampshire and when Paulsen was seen for 30 seconds on an old Doris Day movie earlier in February, NBC agreed to give equal time to Representative Paul N. Mc-

Closkey of California and Representative John M. Ashbrook of Ohio. They each got 30 seconds on NBC's *Saturday Night at the Movies* on March 4, 1972.

Woody, in San Francisco, had nothing to say. His spokesman was his agent and executive producer, Charles Joffe. "Both Woody and I think it's a shame that a program that was done entirely as entertainment should be the source of such controversy," Joffe declared. "We brought it to public television because we thought there we would have complete freedom. But we don't intend to make a big issue of it."

What Joffe might have said but didn't was that Woody had made exactly $135 on the show, minimum scale for actors. He had donated his services as writer and director because he thought public television worthy of support and he naturally thought that, outside the commercial restraints of the three networks, he would have complete artistic freedom.

"I thought it was an innocuous but insulting show. It lacked maybe great political depth or insight, but it was a funny half hour," Woody said. "Those people who are against the administration would have loved it, and those who were for the administration would have written me off as a crackpot. It was all so silly. It wasn't Jonathon Swift. If the show had gone on as scheduled, it would have passed unnoticed."

But the PBS brouhaha and earlier criticisms of Nixon had earned Woody a secure place on the not-yet-released Nixon enemies list, which may turn out to be one of the most prestigious and coveted awards of the twentieth century.

* * * * * *

February, 1972 also saw the publication of *Getting Even*, Woody's first collection of *New Yorker* pieces. Actually, of the seventeen brief comic essays in the book, only ten had appeared originally in *The New Yorker*. Several had appeared in other publications and several others were appearing for the first time in *Getting Even*. Random House was the publisher.

Woody's subject matter ranged over a wide variety of cultural and literary icons. he satirized everything he found ridiculous and what he found most ridiculous were the ideas, customs, literary styles and philosophical positions that everybody else automatically paid homage to.

In *Getting Even*, Woody's targets include:

The Kafka industry: *"Venal & Sons has at last published the long-awaited first volume of Metterling's laundry lists (The Collected Laundry Lists of Hans Metterling, Vol. 1, 437 pp., plus XXXII-page introduction; indexed; $18.75), with an erudite commentary by the noted Metterling scholar Gunther Eisenbud. The decision to publish this work separately, before the completion of the immense four-volume oeuvre, is both welcome and intelligent, for this obdurate and sparkling book will instantly lay to rest the unpleasant rumors that Venal & Sons, having reaped rich rewards from the Metterling novels, play, and notebooks, diaries, and letters, was merely in search of continued profits from the same lode."*

Pop journalism: *"Identifying criminals is up to each of us. Usually they can be recognized by their large cufflinks and their failure to stop eating when the man sitting next to them is hit by a falling anvil."*

Course descriptions in college catalogues: *"Introduction to Psychology: The theory of human behavior. Why some men are called 'lovely individuals' and why there are others you just want to pinch. Is there a split between mind and body, and, if so, which is better to have? Aggression and rebellion are discussed . . . Special consideration is given to a study of consciousness as opposed to unconsciousness, with many helpful hints on how to remain conscious."*

Hemingway: *"That winter, Alice Toklas, Picasso, and myself took a villa in the south of France. I was then working on what I felt was a major American novel but the print was too small and I couldn't get through it."*

The Dashiell Hammett-Raymond Chandler hardboiled detective novel: Woody's protagonist, Kaiser Lupowitz, has been hired to find God. He immediately hustles over to see Rabbi Itzhak Wiseman, who owes Lupowitz a favor.

KAISER: You ever see Him?

RABBI: Me? Are you kidding? I'm lucky I get to see my grandchildren.

KAISER: Then how do you know he exists?

RABBI: How do I know? What kind of question is that? Could I get a suit like this for fourteen dollars if there was no one up there? Here, feel a gabardine—how can you doubt?

KAISER: You got nothing more to go on?

RABBI: Hey—what's the Old Testament? Chopped liver? How do you think Moses got the Israelites out of Egypt? With a smile and a tap dance? Believe me, you don't part the Red Sea with some gismo from Korvette's. It takes power.

* * * * * *

Woody Allen was also perfectly willing to satirize his own artistic idols. In *Death Knocks*, Woody spins off a brief play from his hero Ingmar Bergman's film *The Seventh Seal*, a somber tale set in Medieval times in which Death plays chess with one of his imminent victims, a knight.

Woody's version is set in the present. The hapless victim is Nat Ackerman, a 57-year-old dress manufacturer, who doesn't want to die because, among other things, he has just merged with Modiste Originals. Death agrees to play gin rummy with Nat who is trying to win another day of life. Death loses. Nat wins an extra day plus $28.00. Nat demands that death pay up.

DEATH: Listen, I need that money.

NAT: Why should you need money?

DEATH: What are you talking about? You're going to the Beyond.

NAT: So?

DEATH: So where's gas? Where's tolls?

NAT: We're going by car!

Woody's comic essays sometimes ring with faint overtones of Max Schulman, S.J. Perelman and Robert Benchley. But Woody Allen has a unique gift for spotting the most vulnerable point in any given literary or philosophical genre, in any bit of received wisdom. Then he zeroes in on the absurdity with laser-like precision:

"A modified form of the Hunger Strike for those whose political convictions are not quite so radical is giving up chives. This small gesture, when used properly, can greatly influence a government and it is well known that Mahatma

Gandhi's insistence on eating his salads untossed shamed the British Government into many concessions."

"Allen is a marvel of a willing and hard-working writer," according to Roger Angell, his editor at *The New Yorker*. "The first things he submitted to us were funny, but not really written: one heard a stand-up comic—good jokes, but just jokes. Allen has made himself into an accomplished writer."

Robert Benchley was a *New Yorker* writer who moved from writing to performing, just as Woody Allen had done in the early Sixties. Benchley invented a comic device known as the Blind Explanation ("There is no such place as Budapest."), which Woody very effectively adapted to his comic purposes: *"All of literature is a footnote to Faust. I have no idea what I mean by that."*

"Benchley has become a new idol to me," Woody said. "Perhaps because everybody else also imitates Perelman's complicated style, I've tried to get simpler, like Benchley, and to write about subjects that really interest me."

* * * * * *

As soon as Woody finished filming *Play It Again, Sam*, he immediately returned his attention to *Everything You Always Wanted to Know about Sex but Were Afraid to Ask*. He had begun working on *Sex* before filming *Sam* in San Francisco. And now, after a three-month hiatus, he was glad to be back directing the seven sketches to which to had reduced Reuben's book. By the time Woody was finished writing, there was very little left of Reuben's book.

"I'd never do an adaptation, so I've thrown out the contents and based the script on the title. It's highly sexual but crazy. I think it's the first real sex comedy. I don't call movies like *Pillow Talk* or *It Happened One Night* sex comedies. I call them romantic comedies. I don't think anyone has ever really done a sex comedy. I mean something like a Marx Brothers comedy. No one has ever tackled sex in that way. First of all, because sex is taboo. People are afraid to make fun of it. I want to do it in a broad Rabelaisian way. Unabashedly. It will be a big knock-down, drag-out thing so that people can go and really have a big belly laugh out of sex;

and not small and sort of sneaky and dirty so people will feel embarrassed to laugh. It's as if the Marx Brothers were turned loose at Masters and Johnson.

"I'm talking about real sex, about sex unashamedly and unequivocally; everything from achieving orgasm to homosexuality and prostitution. All those rampant sexual subjects treated in an extremely broad, surrealistic way.

"I may never get another date," Woody added.

The rights to David Reuben's book had originally been acquired by Elliott Gould and Jack Brodsky. Several writers had attempted to turn the unwieldy property into a screenplay without success.

One night Woody was watching television at home with a couple of friends. Reuben was on a talk show promoting his book. One of the guests observed that the only person who could make a movie out of *Everything You Always Wanted to Know. . .* was Woody Allen. Possibly because the idea was so bizarre, Woody was intrigued.

"No one has ever tackled a sexual satire before. We've had loads of lousy pornography about sex which is a subject taken far too seriously by most people, but it has been virtually untouched in a humorous vein."

Gould and Brodsky agreed to sell the rights to Woody if they could be listed as producers. Financial terms were agreed on, the papers were signed and soon the project was underway. Woody spent literally a few minutes glancing through Reuben's book then began writing his own version.

"Frankly, the movie couldn't have been made until now. The industry and public weren't ready. The censorship on films was too tough," Woody said. "Although there is no nudity in the movie, situations are presented with some very intimate aspects.

"Most people are interested in seeing a real sex comedy. Of course, there's a lot more sex today, and there's perversion for the entire family in this one," Woody added.

Among the topics covered were homosexuality, impotence, frigidity, perversion and the validity of sex clinic research. The actors Woody recruited included Tony Randall, Burt Reynolds, John Carradine, Gene Wilder and Lynn Redgrave. Most of them appeared in only one sketch. Woody, of course, appeared in several segments, playing a sperm cell, a spider, a court jester and a sexual loser named Victor Shakapopolis.

The most successful of the sketches answers the question *What Happens During Ejaculation?* (The questions precede each sketch in plain white letters on a black background, the question format being virtually the only entity that survives intact the transition from book to movie.)

We are taken inside a man's libidinal control center and find that it bears an astonishing resemblance to the control center of a missile launch operation. Tony Randall, assisted by Burt Reynolds, is in charge of the center while in the lower regions a team of hard-hats labor manfully to produce an erection. (You wouldn't think it would be that hard . . .) Woody plays Sperm #2 who doesn't really want to be shot into . . . well, wherever.

Are Transvestites Homosexual? tells the story of Tess and Sam, a fairly typical middle-aged Jewish couple. The only jarring note in their marriage is that unbeknownst to Tess, Sam likes to wear frilly women's clothing. Unfortunately, Tess has invited their future in-laws to dinner and even more unfortunately, they catch Sam arrayed in all his glory.

Not to worry. Tess is a loving wife, understanding and helpful. *"Sam, we've been together for years. I love you. You love me. You could have come to me and said 'Tess, I have a diseased mind. I'm a sick individual. I need help. I need treatment. I'm unfit to function with normal, decent people.' I'd have understood."*

In *What Is Sodomy?* Gene Wilder plays a Jackson Heights general practitioner who falls madly, carelessly, rhapsodically in love with an Armenian sheep named Daisy. He throws caution to the winds. Soon he is carrying her into hotels in broad daylight and ordering caviar and Champagne (for him) and grass (for her). Finally, he talks her into fulfilling one of his dearest fantasies: she dons a black garter belt and stockings for their lovemaking.

In another episode, with Woody as the court jester feverishly trying to unlock Lynn Redgrave's chastity belt, he says, *"I must think of something quickly, because before you know it the Renaissance will be here and we'll all be painting."*

But *Everything You Always Wanted to Know about Sex*

but Were Afraid to Ask got mixed reviews and even long-time Woody Allen fans were disappointed in the movie. It was strained and had to work entirely too hard to get its laughs. Woody agreed that "a fraction of an inch left or right can kill a joke." He also noted that comedy is a delicate thing and comedy audiences are unpredictable.

"People would come up to me and say, 'I loved the fifth episode . . . but the third and the first were the worst.' Some people said they adored it. Other people said it was in bad taste. There is no way you can think of pleasing people. You have to do the film you want. Comedy is so ephemeral. It is so relational and so dependent on how the audience feels."

All of which is no doubt true, but *Sex* was still a disappointment. Some of his most ardent admirers consider *Sex* to be Woody Allen's failure.

It was a month for failure on other fronts. The presidential campaign of North Dakota Senator George McGovern suffered a crippling blow when it was discovered that his running mate, Missouri Senator Thomas Eagleton, had once been hospitalized for "nervous exhaustion". The entire incident was handled badly, from McGovern's failure to thoroughly check out Eagleton's background to the vacillation Mc-Govern showed when the news broke. Finally, Eagleton was asked to leave the ticket. There was bitterness on both sides.

Of all the presidential candidates that tumultuous year, Woody preferred Benjamin Spock, but supported McGovern because he knew Spock's candidacy was little more than a gesture. But Woody was vocal in his disgust over the Eagleton affair. "It's a reflection on the immaturity of the American public. Our sense of what a presidential or vice-presidential candidate should be is infantile in its expectations. We want perfect, emasculated, uninteresting types with no signs of human weakness about them. All that happens is that the guys who get into office lie and hide those sorts of facts," Woody said. He felt there was a connection between the voters' passion for mediocrity and the leveling influence of television.

"Safety and sterility is what you get when you watch television," he said. "It's our inability to bear any kind of deviation when there is dependence on a mass response. Comedians get a lot of flak in this way. We're constantly under the gun—

from the blandest of us to someone like Lenny Bruce. We're constantly fighting in the movies and on television. It's always: 'Take this joke out, take that joke out.'

"The standards set by the entertainment industry are the result of having no intelligent standards at all," Woody added. "I'm against censorship of any form."

In spite of his opposition to political taboos on television, Woody continued to insist he was not a topical comedian. "A comedian has no obligation to be relevant," Woody said. "He has an obligation to be funny. It's too easy to do jokes about topical things. If I went on television and did a couple of Eagleton jokes . . . sure I'd get a laugh."

* * * * * *

Woody had become the foremost American comic of his time, and certainly the most versatile. Nobody else but Woody Allen had yet managed to get gigs at both Caesar's Palace and *The New Yorker*. Not surprisingly, he was frequently compared to four clowns from an earlier, far less sophisticated but much more vigorous, comic era: Groucho and Harpo Marx, Charlie Chaplin and Buster Keaton. Woody had obviously given the matter considerable thought. "The common thread that ties the other four and me is probably the obsession and compulsion to try to elicit the laughter from any situation—and the sense of suffering when it doesn't come. Comedians are supposed to be sad people, the myth says. I don't know if it's true or not. It probably is, based on my observations. The only thing I feel in common with these four is that our lives have been pretty much dedicated to getting laughs. That is the kernel of our creative existence. You know comedians don't really age . . . If we all sat in a room talking, we'd probably all recognize one another's feelings.

"I know Groucho fairly well. Generally, I just like to listen to him talk. He's such a fount of insights and witticisms . . . Often comedians take their work much less seriously than other people do. There's a tendency to look at my movies and to over-analyze them. And that's also true about the people who write about Keaton and the Marx Brothers. When all we really are, are entertainers trying to make funny movies.

Sometimes we succeed. Sometimes we fail. But it's never the heavy, intellectual nonsense written about us. All I want people to do is laugh at the movie. If they don't think it's funny, I'll buy that, too.

"All the reams written about these four comedians! These people functioned in early years when none of that heavy-handed commentary occurred. Each of them made a whole slew of movies; some were funny, some were not. You had a following, and they were for you, and you tried not to disappoint them . . . Pictures are things you should be able to see for twenty-five or fifty cents. You should be able to see them free—or for very little. Eventually it's going to cost $12 to see a movie! A fellah is going to look down dazed and say, 'Hey! I can't take my wife to the movies!' Movies are going to be moribund—like the theater. I believe the theater is moribund; and one of the things about it is that, when my mother and father want to go see a show, it costs them sixteen or seventeen dollars. In order to have a vital theater you have to support all sorts of things, you have to see all sorts of things.

"I see myself in kind of the typical American tradition of comedy: physically amusing-looking and kind of typical—fearful, brash. These are all things I impute to the American comedian. Chaplin, Bob Hope, Groucho—I think I'm in that tradition. I'm not saying I'm as strong as they are . . .

"I get a lot of Buster Keaton. People abroad and in this country have drawn analogies between Keaton and myself. This came as a surprise to me. I have to make it very clear here: I'm not talking about degrees of skill. I don't want to compare myself to Keaton or to any of these others . . . I never saw a Keaton film until about two years ago. I've seen one, *The General*. It's wonderful. But people say I remind them of him. I mean that in the most general way. I mean, I'm more like Keaton than I am like W.C. Fields. Fields is one of my particular favorites. He was a total original, incredibly unsentimental. It's a reward to one to be able to see the world through Fields' eyes every now and then. It's such a refreshing and hilarious way of looking at life . . .

"But getting back to Keaton: it always surprises me to hear there's any trace of him in me. I can only think of two things. There may be the most remote kind of impassivity about our faces, and there's a slightly sophisticated quality about Keaton's work, as opposed to Chaplin's, who's broader. My work has a slight intellectual component. Keaton had that. He wasn't quite as music-hall as Chaplin. Keaton had an exceptionally beautiful face. Chaplin also had an unusually beautiful face. Keaton had more of that famous impassive quality about his face, which might be mistaken for sadness: it's certainly unsmiling.

"I have, by nature, an enormously sad face. I'm not a smiler. If you didn't know I was a comic, I would be a study in sadness. My face is naturally sad, because it's drawn and my eyes are droopy. It's easy to hate yourself.

"Groucho was unparalled as a movie comedian. He did everything funny. He spoke funny and walked funny and danced funny and sang funny. He had total command, like a great musical virtuoso who has total command of his instrument and is flawless. Thoroughly original. (There's) nothing to compare with Groucho Marx. He's incredibly American in the sense that Louis Armstrong and baseball are American. He's a biting, cynical, utterly irreverent, wisecracking, surrealistic clown: one of the great joys of the world of entertainment. He's a national heritage.

"I'm crazy about Charlie Chaplin. I wish I had eyes like (his) . . . deep sockets, dark. I like Chaplin better than Keaton. Most of my intellectual friends frown upon that estimation. Chaplin took risks. And frequently those risks didn't come off; and he came out as pompous, maudlin, and embarrassing. When those risks did pay off, then I don't think anybody came close to him. Of all comedies ever made, *City Lights* is the best; his best, probably anyone's best. He walked the tightrope between his sentimentality and his humor, and maybe came a little too close to sentimentality once or twice in it; but he managed to maintain the proportions, so that he has in this picture some of the greatest comic moments ever. It's one of the few broad comedy pictures that packs an emotional wallop. The prizefight scene is as great as any comic segment in any picture. The end, the last two minutes—shattering, if you're willing to let your defenses down and go with it. Treat yourself to a moment of weakness . . . I've never met Chaplin. I could have. I don't really like meeting idols very much—not because they disappoint, I kinda look at them open-mouthed. I want to keep certain people distant, so I can continue to worship.

"Harpo . . . he was absolutely brilliant. Incidentally, he was one of those comedians with a stunningly beautiful face. His, Charlie's, Keaton's . . . almost feminine. Harpo has incredible wit in his pantomime, which almost no other purely physical, nonverbal comedian has. There's a heavy intellectual element in his work that makes it fascinating. His style is that of the lowdown; but his instincts for getting laughter are so intellectual—that combination is fascinating. He'll hand his leg to a beautiful girl to hold: that's enormously witty to do. He's physical with incredible cleverness. In the Marx Brothers movies that were well written, by George S. Kaufman or Harry Ruby or S.J. Perelman, Groucho stands out so much you can't see anybody else. But in some of the later movies, where the writing fell off and Groucho isn't supplied with his usual top-level remarks, Harpo is unfailingly funny—incredibly. And again, like Groucho, unbelievably American . . . Harpo's choice of costume . . . Groucho's choice . . . nothing in the world looks like Groucho and Harpo. Other comedians—there's always a similarity, roughly; but those two Marx brothers were just incredible!"

And what did Groucho himself have to say about all of this? "They say Allen got something from the Marx Brothers. He didn't. He's an original. The best. The funniest."

chapter 5

Woody Allen:

Musician

ALL THROUGH THE NIGHTCLUB YEARS, during his Broadway and Hollywood debuts, Woody Allen had been a closet clarinetist, usually spending an hour a day practicing so he wouldn't lose his "lip".

Woody's music had begun when he was fifteen. Inspired by the legendary Sidney Bechet, Woody taught himself to play the soprano saxophone. Then Woody heard George Lewis and knew right away that he wanted to learn the clarinet as well. He bought all of Lewis' available records and listened to them over and over, until he was able to play along with Lewis and other members of his group. To this day, Woody cannot read music.

For years, Woody had taken his clarinet and stereo with him when he played out-of-town club dates. But he had never played in a real band. All that changed in 1968, when he was in San Francisco filming *Take the Money and Run*. Turk Murphy invited Woody to sit in with his band at Earthquake McGoon's.

"I got to play with Pops Foster and Wild Bill Davison and other good musicians," Woody recalled. Once he came out of the closet, there was no stopping him. "Then, in New Orleans, they let me play in a street parade with Percy Humphrey's band. And I played in Congo Square with Punch Miller, Cie

Frazier, Chester Zardis—all the people I'd heard about. I was awestruck meeting them."

The jazz clarinetist that Woody now respects most is Albert Burbank. "When I sat in with him in New Orleans, he intimidated me," Woody said. "He's got the most unearthly, beautiful sound. The thing that always gets me the most about a clarinetist is the tone."

The next logical step was for Woody to organize his own band, which is just what he did early in 1970. With several friends, including his writing collaborator Marshall Brickman, who were also jazz buffs, Woody formed the New Orleans Funeral and Ragtime Orchestra. By the time they had recruited several other avocational jazz musicians in the New York area the group had seven members: John Bucher, a stockbroker, on cornet; Dick Dreiwitz, a teacher, on trombone; Barbara Dreiwitz, Dick's wife and at that time a graduate student in music at Hunter College, on tuba; Brickman, then head writer on the Dick Cavett show, on banjo; Dick Miller, a college English teacher, on piano; and Jay Duke, then working in a radio store in Montclair, N.J., on drums.

In October, the group began playing once-a-week Wednesday night gigs at Barney Google's on East 86th Street. As a bandleader, Woody kept a very low profile. And he invariably left his comedian's hat at home when he was wearing his clarinetist hat. "I just come in and play and leave," Woody said. "I'm not too funny, normally, anyway. That's a distinct Kafkaesque quality about me."

The entire repertoire of The New Orleans Funeral and Ragtime Orchestra consisted of old-style New Orleans jazz, a style not much in vogue in recent decades; but Woody was playing for love, not fashion. "It's a limited art form," he said, "one you have to cultivate a taste for. What the public wants is the commercial stuff—Al Hirt, or the Dukes of Dixieland. People don't turn out in great numbers to hear us."

Still, when the group debuted at Barney Google's, they got very good notices from *The New York Times*: "Mr. Allen's style on clarinet shows traces of his two favorites, George Lewis and Albert Burbank, and there are moments when one can detect echoes of Ted Lewis. He is a confident, surprisingly adept performer who holds his own with a band that rolls through tightly knit, lusty ensemble passages, led by Mr. Bucher's strong, singing cornet and carried by a powerful rhythm section that gets frequent exhilirating boots from Mrs. Dreiwitz's tuba."

Not bad for a bunch of amateurs.

A few months later, Woody's band played a joint benefit concern with Eric Night on the Moog Synthesizer at the Village Gate. Proceeds went to the Gardens Nursery School-Kindergarten.

The New Orleans Funeral and Ragtime Orchestra played several New York clubs, finally settling into regular Monday night performances at Michael's Pub, a stylish East Side saloon. "I don't permit any advertising about where I play," Woody says. "It's no big deal. I'm as happy just sitting in my own living room and playing as I am in a club. Even now, I play along with recordings every day. If I don't play for a day or two, I'm afraid I'll lose it all.

"I've been to New Orleans a couple of times to play in jazz festivals," Woody has said. "I'd love to move down there and do all my writing. If I could earn my living as a musician, it would be great, but I don't think I could."

Woody's clarinet dates from the late nineteenth century, which is also the period when many of the tunes in his repertoire were written and achieved their first popularity. The tone and fingering on Woody's instrument are slightly different from modern instruments. "The old bands often played sharp or flat," Woody said. "In New Orleans style the emphasis is on how you treat the tune. You don't notice the technique."

He fears that his fame as a comedian interferes with an honest assessment of his work, especially by other jazz musicians. "Nobody's ever commented . . . ever said a thing to me about my playing that I thought was sincere," Woody said.

But one jazz player who has heard Woody numerous times says he is highly thought of by other musicians. "He's a tremendously authentic player in that narrow and specific area of New Orleans jazz. If he had been born black and 100 years ago, he would have been a revered clarinet player—and he'd have starved like the rest of them."

* * * * * *

Possibly the most enjoyable and satisfying gig that Woody ever played was in New Orleans in the summer of 1973 sitting in with the Preservation Hall Jazz Band, a group that counts among its members most of the surviving greats of the golden era of New Orleans Jazz: Chester Zardis, Emanuel Sayles, Josiah "Cie" Frazier, Percy Humphrey and Sing Miller.

Preservation Hall is small (about 40 by 20 feet) and noticeably crumbling from age. There are no seats, only benches. When they're full, the jazz fans who regularly pack the place are happy to stand. The acoustics are superb.

Woody played three full sessions with the band. Sometimes he would have to listen for a few seconds before he knew what they were playing. Then he would unobstrusively join in. "He has a wonderful ear," Percy Humphrey said later. "He did what you should do when you sit with another man's band. He played along with what we played. He didn't try to be a celebrity."

This time, however, Woody was combining business and pleasure. Through United Artists, Woody was paying the Preservation Hall Jazz Band $12,000 to provide background music for Woody's new film, *Sleeper*. He described it as his "view of the future. It takes place 200 years from now. It has science fiction, romantic scenes, slapstick, chase scenes; it's an action love story. I'm using New Orleans jazz for the background music because I didn't want to use the stereotyped Moog synthesizer music usually used for futuristic things. I want the music to play against the story. I also like the idea of playing behind myself to complement my playing on the screen."

It had taken Woody longer to make *Sleeper* than any of his other movies. And he had taken more risks.

chapter 6

Time Travel

WOODY ALLEN DESERVES CREDIT for always wanting to extend himself professionally and artistically, even though his willingness to risk isn't always successful, in comic terms if not at the box-office. *Sleeper* is different from anything he had ever done. Woody's humor had traditionally depended on its attachment to modern, urban, hip culture. In this sense, it had a certain coziness. To transplant this comic sensibility into a future time locale where none of the tried and true associations would be operational is not the act of a cautious man. It may, however, be the act of a man who is both artistically bold and increasingly self-confident.

Woody first had the idea of making a science fiction spoof when he was shooting *Everything You Always Wanted to Know about Sex but Were Afraid to Ask.* One day Woody was not afraid to ask assistant director Fred Gallo, "How much do you think it would cost to build a futuristic town?"

Gallo's reply was succinct and to the point. "Millions," he said. Gallo had a pessimistic view of science fiction projects; he felt they were among the most difficult subjects to put on film. "There are four things to stay away from in movies: boats and water, animals, kids and futurism."

Woody was not deterred. He had always, after all, indulged himself with numerous surreal moments in his films. In *Bananas*, for example, he had a quartet of elderly string players performing at a state dinner . . . in mime. Impeccably dressed in formal clothing, they passionately pulled their imaginary bows over the non-existent cellos, violins, violas.

And we suddenly realize how close to absurdity hovers the most dignified of human actions.

Now he would simply make a movie that was surreal from beginning to end. As soon as the editing of *Sex* was completed, Woody called Marshall Brickman and the two of them began to toss ideas back and forth. Brickman and Allen are both accomplished gag writers and had been off-and-on collaborators since 1969 when they had written a movie called *The Filmmaker* which, as it happens, no one wanted to produce. Brickman had been head writer for Johnny Carson in the Sixties. When Woody called him in the summer of 1972 to see if he wanted to help write a science fiction send-up, Brickman was producer and creative director for Dick Cavett.

By fall, they had tossed out several ideas and settled on a basic plot line: Miles Monroe (Woody Allen), the proprietor of The Happy Carrot Health Food Restaurant in Greenwich Village, needs a minor ulcer operation. He is admitted to St. Vincent Hospital, is prepared for surgery and goes under the anesthetic without a qualm. After all, what could possibly go wrong? Everything, it seems. When the good doctors at St. Vincent realize they can't finish their job properly, they wrap Miles in aluminum foil and freeze him, much as you'd wrap a leftover leg of lamb and pop it in the freezer until you can figure out what to do with it.

Miles wakes up 200 years later to an America that has become a police state full of real robots that function as servants and human robots that have lost the ability to function intellectually and sexually. The women are frigid, the men are impotent and people have sex by entering the Orgasmitron, a machine that looks like an over-sized water heater. One steps inside, and moments later the task is accomplished without muss, fuss or the necessity of removing one's clothes.

America is ruled in 2173 by The Leader, a man whose television style bears an uncanny resemblance to the game show hosts of the 1970's. The Leader's secret police, who bear an uncanny resemblance to the Keystone Cops, are soon after Woody. He has taken refuge disguised as a robot in the home of the lovely Luna Schlosser, a poet in the tradition of Rod McKuen, who gets her poetic metaphors mixed up because she can never remember whether caterpillars turn into butterflies or the other way around.

Brickman won't tell which parts of *Sleeper* are his. "All I can say is that when you collaborate, you are both responsible for everything. You never know when one person will make the other person think of something. The early parts are hard. You try not to make any big mistakes, to paint yourself into a corner."

Marshall Brickman and Woody Allen have remarkably similar comic styles. Brickman has also begun publishing short comic essays in *The New Yorker*. Without the unobstrusive *New Yorker* byline at the end of the piece, one could easily think Brickman's casuals had been written by Woody Allen.

They bounce lines off each other like two facets of the same comic phenomenon. Recently, Brickman and Woody were walking together in mid-town Manhattan.

ALLEN: Isn't that what's-his-name, you know, the agent?

BRICKMAN: Oh, yeah, I didn't recognize him without his mustache.

ALLEN: I hear he had a bad divorce.

BRICKMAN: Apparently his wife won the mustache.

ALLEN: I think she sued for the whole face and settled for the mustache.

* * * * * *

The filming of *Sleeper* began in February, 1973, in Denver. This location had been chosen because Woody had seen a suburban Denver house of avant-garde design in a shelter magazine. White and nearly round in shape—one side had a flat facade—the house stood on a pedestal and was perfect for the futuristic ambience Woody hoped to create in *Sleeper*.

The movie was budgeted at $2 million and seven weeks' shooting time. When filming was finally completed, it had taken 14 weeks; the cost overrun was $1.1 million, bringing the final budget for *Sleeper* to $3.1 million.

The reason for the delays was that Woody had become much more knowledgeable about the art and craft of moviemaking and was willing to make expensive set and costume changes and to relentlessly keep shooting until he got exactly what he wanted, a position that, at least in the world of film, means enormous inflation of costs. If a writer wants to rewrite a chapter in her current novel, the only out-of-pocket expense is for paper and a bit of typewriter ribbon. But a director who wants to reshoot a scene in a movie must often pay an extra two or three days' salary to upwards of 40 well-paid technicians.

Most of the exteriors were shot near Denver, Boulder and other Rocky Mountain locations. Then the crew traveled back to Los Angeles where the interiors were filmed along with a few added exteriors in the Monterey Peninsula area.

In an apparently conscious effort to pay homage to the comic styles of his heroes Groucho, Harpo and Charlie Chaplin, Woody wanted *Sleeper* to depend more on slapstick and sight gags than on the kind of verbal, intellectual humor that had predominated in his three earlier movies. It is the *idea* of Howard Cosell in *Bananas* doing a play-by-play on the Assassination of the Week that is basically funny, rather than the execution of the idea. That is, one laughs on hearing the idea without ever seeing it on the screen. But, in *Sleeper*, when Woody is in a motorized wheelchair that has suddenly come to life, it will only be funny if Woody *makes* it funny. It's not especially amusing in and of itself.

Sleeper abounds in slapstick, including Woody being intimidated by a pudding that won't stop and has to be beaten into submission with a broom, several Keystone Cops chase sequences, and Woody dressed up as one of the servant robots, complete with chalk-white make-up, a speaker for a mouth and, of course, the trademark of his glasses. For his scenes as a robot, Woody developed a special walk, reminiscent of Chaplin's innocent waddle.

Still, there is plenty of intellectual humor and most of the time it works better than the slapstick which seems strained and forced. When Miles asks the doctors who defrost him what caused the nuclear holocaust that nearly wiped out civilization shortly after he was put in the freezer, they reply that, as nearly as they can determine, a man named Albert Shanker got hold of a nuclear warhead. Shanker is the president of the American Federation of Teachers in New York and was a key figure in the bitter Ocean Hill-Brownsville teachers' strike in the Sixties.

The joke was pure self-indulgence on Woody's part. New Yorkers loved it, but the rest of the country was no doubt mystified.

Miles also discovers the medical profession in 2173 is recommending steak, mashed potatoes and fudge to those who want to attain optimum health and well-being. Physicians are also recommending smoking. Gives a quick energy pick-up, they say. The medics also want to know about a man named Nixon. If records on the man exist, they have not yet been found. "We have a theory that he might once have been President of the United States, but that he did something horrendous." (*Sleeper*, of course, was shot during 1973, the year of Watergate, but was released well before Representative Peter Rodino's House impeachment panel had begun hearings and before Nixon's resignation in August, 1974.)

Other delightful moments in *Sleeper* include a brief sketch with Diane Keaton playing Stanley Kowalski to Woody Allen's Blanche DuBois; and an operating room sequence in which Woody and Diane are attempting to clone the rest of The Leader from the one fragment of his person that still exists: his nose.

"*Sleeper* is a picture every kid in America could see," Woody observed. "It's a picture that every kid from five or six to thirteen could see and find funny. It's exactly the kind of picture that I used to see as a kid and love. It bothers me that I would be confined to intellectual humor. Chaplin had some very hip jokes in his stuff. I'm tired of being thought of as special for that Third Avenue crowd."

Woody Allen's sense of the way movies have shaped all our minds was underscored when he discovered that Jack Solomon, *Sleeper*'s soundman, was the soundman for a 1940's movie called *Tom, Dick and Harry*.

". . . I remember in 1944 or '43—I was only eight years old—standing in front of a tailor shop in Brooklyn. They used to have these cards in the windows advertising the week's movies. And I remember seeing *Tom, Dick and Harry* advertised and saying, 'I can't wait to see that.' It was one of those things that became a part of my conscious, because I lived in the movies and identified with that. And then here I am working with Jack Solomon and he's my soundman now. It's such a weird feeling. Twenty, thirty years ago; one of the reasons I'm in movies today is because of that."

Sleeper went over both its dollars and time budgets because, in many respects, Woody was feeling his way and couldn't rely on quick set-ups using previous techniques and formats. Often, he would try several ways of doing a scene until he'd managed to get on film something that "felt" right.

"*Sleeper* was pure torture to do," he said. "I found myself working over and over on one particular scene, the kind of scene where I'm seen dangling from a ladder, and, maybe out of incredible planning, I might get a minute of film."

Woody said that he had wanted *Sleeper* to look like "a great big cartoon . . . cute and funny." One of the key elements in getting this look were the robot-servants. He wanted them to be believable as real comic robots and not just as actors-playing-robots. But after the final comic design was agreed on, Woody then had to create the way in which he wanted the robots to move. Finally, there was the problem of getting Woody into one of the robots' tuxedos.

"You can imagine—knowing me—how I felt about wearing tails. I'd like to do a film like I'm dressed now, a film based in New York. Anything so I don't have to dress. I have very low aesthetic ideals. Clothes are not the things that motivate me. That's why I loved doing *Play It Again, Sam* on Broadway. I didn't have to dress at all. I could leave home dressed in my normal clothes and walk right out on stage just as I was. All I had to worry about was being neat. I was funnier because of it. When you're in a space suit in 100-degree temperatures, you really suffer. You can't wait to get out of it, and so you only do one take. Consequently, you compromise your work," Woody declared.

No one, however, who has ever worked with him believes that Woody Allen would compromise on anything he felt to be even slightly important. He is reputed to have a relentless stubbornness when it comes to doing things his own way. Woody and his crew had originally been scheduled for one week's shooting in and around Denver. But Woody insisted on so many set changes and script changes that it stretched to one month.

Woody tired of living in a Denver motel and said about halfway through the Colorado tour of duty that he would love a week-end of "pure pleasure": like watching a couple of old Bob Hope movies. "I think Bob Hope is fantastic . . . especially some of his early films like *Paleface* and *Monsieur Beaucaire*. What's funny about Hope over the years is not the lines, although they're good, too. He's just a funny guy. He's writing, in the editing. It's a tough racket." Over the years, he has been dismayed to see television replace movies as *the* mass medium. "Movie-making has become a high-pressure business with a low survival rate. I'm for turning out a comedy every year. Some of the other comedians could do it, too. I wish we could just keep turning them out. But you just can't work that way when you feel you are on the line every time."

Woody's three one-acts on sex, love and death, however, have not yet made it to Broadway. The reason why can possibly be deduced from something he said just after *Love and Death* had been released: ". . . Getting money in the theater is different (from getting money for films.) Even though the amount is much less, it's easier to go in and get $3,000,000 to make a film than it is to get $250,000 for a play. You can write for the theater with reasonable ease if you're willing to write those kinds of plays that are commercially promising. So if I wrote a play that was basically a simple comedy with a lot of laughs and not too big a cast and not too complex a set requirement, there would be no problem getting it on at all. But as soon as you try to write something different or interesting, less commercially acceptable, then you run into problems. So who needs it?"

Who, indeed, when it is possible to spend nine months in Europe making yet another movie with the winsome Diane Keaton?

* * * * * *

In *Sleeper*, Woody Allen travels two hundred years into the future. In *Love and Death*, he travels one hundred years into the past. Specifically, the Russian past of Tolstoy, Dostoevski and similar tortured Slavs whose intense absorption with the mysteries of love and death, God and infinity, moral righteousness and psychological angst was at least equal to Woody Allen's. They may even have been more intensely preoccupied with these issues than Woody. After all, they didn't have to worry about muggers in Central Park, sidewalks befouled by dog excrement or the box-office receipts in Omaha.

Love and Death is the story of Boris Grushenko (Woody Allen), a philosophizing coward, who is in love with his

got a funny jut to his jaw and a silly look on his face. His whole attitude, his behavior—the man's hilarious."

Sleeper kept Woody Allen away from New York for nearly a year. That, in itself, was one of the biggest drawbacks involved in writing, directing and acting in his fourth film. Forget the artistic risks, the inflated budget, the technical problems. "I'm a big New York lover despite all its problems. The city has so much going for it. I enjoy the country only if I'm with nice people. Here you don't have to be with nice people to enjoy it. You can be with the muggers."

Woody Allen usually prefers to edit movies after all the film is in the can even though a good many directors will do a rough cut as they go along. But with *Sleeper* so far behind schedule, United Artists' brass persuaded him to let veteran film editor Ralph Rosenblum begin his job before all the scenes were shot. Rosenblum had been with Woody since *Take the Money and Run*, his first film. Based in New York, Rosenblum had edited 17 movies before *Sleeper*, including *The Pawnbroker*, *Fail Safe* and *Long Day's Journey into Night*. He had also edited Mel Brooks' *The Producers*. Rosenblum says there is little difference in his approach to drama or comedy.

"In comedy, there may be more stuff going on—more improvisation," he feels. "You may not be covered from as many angles and you may have to work harder to make a routine succeed.

"A film is written and directed with a point of view. Editing is the realization of that point of view. Once something has been photographed, a new element has been introduced," Rosenblum declares. Each time the photographer rolls the camera, a piece of film is shot which has a beginning, a middle and an end. "In editing, the idea is to take the beginnings and the ends off and make it appear seamless."

Rosenblum said that Woody Allen has an objectivity in the editing room that is rare in most directors. "He's more ruthless than I am," Rosenblum added. "I'll tell him that something is a terrific idea and he'll say, 'You don't get points for ideas,' and he'll throw it out."

As soon as Woody finished shooting, he joined Rosenblum in New York and the two of them worked at the crucial editing chore. In October, Woody flew to New

Orleans where he sat in with the Preservation Hall Jazz Band and spent two days recording their sessions. Rosenblum was waiting for the results back in New York so he could begin scoring the film.

In addition to the music he recorded in Preservation Hall, Woody recorded additional music with his own New Orleans Funeral and Ragtime Orchestra. "All along, I've expected that I would record some of the music with my band when I got back to New York," Woody said. "For some scenes I need to choose music to fit where I'm running, for instance, and with my band I can tell them to play faster or slower, or when I need a break, or a tuba solo, or where I can play a couple of riffs. I can't do that in another man's band. It will be interesting to have a contrast with both bands."

Sleeper was United Artists' Christmas release and even with a $1.1 budget excess bringing total costs to $3.1 million, it was a much less expensive movie than the other studios' Christmas shows: *The Sting* cost $8 million; *Day of the Dolphin* cost $9 million; *The Exorcist* cost $12 million.

Reviews were generally favorable although several critics expressed reservations, primarily concerning the absence of the "humanistic madness" present in all his earlier films except *Sex*. But it hardly mattered. Woody Allen had built an audience that would go see him no matter what the reviews said.

* * * * * *

Even after Woody's success as the screenwriter for *What's New, Pussycat?* it took Charles Joffe 18 months to get Woody the terms he insisted on for his next movie project. Woody Allen had decided that he was not going to write any more scripts for other people to do with as they chose: he knew their choice would almost certainly involve mangling his work almost beyond recognition. Woody insisted that he would direct and star in any script he might write and that Joffe would produce it. United Artists refused these terms, but finally Joffe was able to make a deal with Palomar Pictures. They gave Woody $1.6 million and complete control. The result? *Take the Money and Run*, which earned back Palomar Pictures' $1.6 million and turned a profit as well.

The success of Woody's first movie gave United Artists second thoughts. Joffe was able to rather quickly negotiate a contract with David Picker, then president of United Artists. Its terms were: $2 million budget per film, total control for Woody once UA had approved the story idea, and a three-picture deal.

Sleeper was the third film in the contract (*Bananas* and *Sex* had been the first two) and the only one to go over budget. All of Woody Allen's films have made money. Of his first four movies, each made more money than the last. They cost $8.7 to produce, grossed $36 million, returning a profit of $10.5 million. (*Play It Again, Sam*, as mentioned earlier, was a Paramount release in which Woody starred but did not direct. *Sam* has grossed well over $11 million.)

A couple of weeks before *Sleeper* was released, Woody signed a new four-picture contract with United Artists. The first movie of the new contract turned out to be *Love and Death*, but first Woody had to spend several months promoting *Sleeper*.

Woody Allen has frequently admitted that no matter what he finds himself doing he always wishes he were doing something else. He once said to fellow *New Yorker* writer and film critic Penelope Gilliatt, "I always think the next thing I do will be fun. Then when I do it I don't like it at all."

Having spent a year making a movie, his thoughts turned to Broadway. He had talked for years of directing three one-act plays on his three favorite obsessions: *Sex, Love* and *Death*. "I would like to appear in the theater again because that's the most fun. You leave your house at 7 o'clock. You go on stage and you get your laughs. The audiences are very nice. They don't drink like they do in night clubs. The curtain comes down about 10:30, and you're free to go. It's very civilized compared to being in films. Films are strenuous, back-breaking work. You go from morning to night with bad hours, bad food. There is that wonderful story about Groucho Marx when he was doing *A Night in Casablanca*. He and Harpo were hanging from the back of an airplane. And he said to Harpo, 'Have you had enough?' And Harpo said 'Yup.'

"It's like a three-dimensional chess game," Woody said "There are so many places you can fail. You can fail in th

cousin, the lovely Sonja (Diane Keaton). But Sonja is in love with Boris' brother Ivan who marries somebody else before going off to fight Napoleon. Sonja then decides she doesn't need love all that much and plans to wed a very rich old man. Unfortunately, he leaves this vale of tears (i.e., dies) before the wedding that would have made Sonja a rich widow within a matter of weeks. So, in a wildly irrational mood, Sonja marries a fishmonger who smells, not surprisingly, of fish. And Sonja begins to take lovers as if she were in an adultery marathon.

Boris, meanwhile, reluctantly goes off to battle the French, accidentally becomes a hero and comes home, his chest full of medals, in triumph. Enter an over-sexed countess who easily seduces Boris. Enter her official lover who challenges Boris to a duel.

Duels were very popular then. Sonja's fishmonger husband has accidentally shot himself while preparing for a duel meant to defend Sonja's somewhat dubious honor. So Sonja says she will marry Boris, convinced he will be shot in her dead husband's place. Miraculously, Boris survives the duel and Sonja reluctantly goes through with the wedding. She and Boris spend a lot of time in bed tossing cliches at each other as if they were beanbags.

In a burst of patriotism, Sonja decides that Boris should assassinate Napoleon. Sonja figures this will stop the French advance into Mother Russia.

Strung on this silly plot are the usual Allen pearls: an obligatory battle scene that pokes fun at the standard epic battle scene a la Hollywood; a scene with a 7-foot Grim Reaper inexplicably dressed in white instead of the usual black; Boris and Sonja's endless going-nowhere discussions on free will and the existence of God which brilliantly parody modern pseudo-intellectuals' half-assed attempts to sound knowledgable.

According to Woody Allen's account in *Esquire* of the filming of *Love and Death*, the production was plagued from the very beginning.

"From the start, the making of Love and Death *was cursed by mysterious, cosmic shenanigans. Probably because the movie is highly critical of God. It implies He doesn't exist, or if He does, He really can't be trusted. (Since coming to this*

conclusion I have twice been nearly struck by lightning and once forced to engage in a long conversation with a theatrical agent.) The truth is, I have always been an agnostic. If there is a God, I reason, why are there such things as famine and daytime television?"

Woody then described his traditional Jewish childhood and his adolescent flirtation with Catholicism, motivated primarily by his curiosity: he wanted to see if he could induce partial paralysis in his father's face . . .

"My relentless questioning of deep moral issues continued for many years. Then, some months ago, as I was looking about for a script idea (I'd rejected the notion of doing Mildred Pierce *with me in the Joan Crawford role), some friends proposed that I do something based on my philosophical obsessions. Great idea, I thought. A comedy about death and one's existence in a godless universe. The commercial possibilities were immediately apparent to me. Sight gags and slapstick sequences about despair and emptiness. Dialogue jokes about anguish and dread. Finality, mortality, human suffering, anxiety. In short, the standard ploys of the professional funnyman. I thanked my friends and told them we must get together and discuss all this more fully at a later date. I suggested we meet just after the next glacial period."*

Woody then turned his time, attention and talents to other script ideas: egg-candling in Peru; a love story between two circus pinheads; a musical about the discovery of negative space. Strangely enough, none of these dynamite concepts would jell . . .

"Finally, feeling the frustration of no progress, I began to feel drawn back to the religious movie. Maybe the subject matter was *heavy, but at least it was a fresh, untried area.*

"I applied pen to paper and came up with a first draft. Several weeks later I found myself in the offices of United Artists' biggest deal-makers, explaining that I had written a comedy about man's alienation in a world of meaningless existence. They had been led to believe—owing to certain memos I'd sent—that I was working on a bedroom farce based on the mistaken identity of two au pair girls and some hens. Imagine their delighted surprise when I read them the script of Love and Death, *with its plot that went from war to*

political assassination, ending with the death of its hero caused by a cruel trick of God. Never having witnessed eight film executives go into cardiac arrest simultaneously, I was quite amused. Regaining their breath, they proceeded to assure me that while they respected the seriousness of the premise, they thought my basic talent lay more in the direction of some of the simpler Three Stooges shorts. Though they agreed that death and atheism were indeed provocative subjects for farce, they said they would call the police if I didn't leave their office and never come back. Invoking the artistic prerogative clause in my contract, a clause which gives me total control over what necktie I can wear while rewriting, I insisted that I go forward with the project. The UA moguls shrewdly asked for some kind of collateral and, placing my right arm in escrow, we came to an agreement."

Filming was scheduled for Paris, Budapest and the Hungarian countryside. Woody and Keaton left for Paris and the mishaps began, in spite of the garlic necklace Keaton was wearing. Woody's luggage turned up in Israel rather than Paris and all his trousers were altered before the missing suitcases were once more in Woody's possession. He and Diane developed a stomach virus. Woody got the flu three times. He accidentally poked Diane in the eye with a violin bow; he backed into a floodlight resulting in second-degree burns. That, as they say, was only the tip of the iceberg.

"During casting and location scouting, actors and desired locations kept dropping out for one reason or another. An actor who'd given a first-rate reading was hired, then broke both legs in an automobile accident. (Later on, an actress who'd filmed half her part fell off a horse and broke her nose.) When good weather was needed, it rained. When rain was needed, it was sunny. The cameraman was Belgian, his crew, French. The underlings were Hungarian, the extras were Russian. I speak only English—and not really all that well. Each shot was chaos. By the time my directions were translated, what should have been a battle scene ended up a dance marathon. In scenes where Keaton and I were supposed to stroll as lovers, Budapest suffered its worst winter in twenty-five years. Throughout these pastoral walks, my lips were so blue they resembled pieces of liver. A lens rented in London proved defective; scenes with thousands of extras on horseback were

so blurry they looked like underwater shots by Jacques Cousteau . . .

"Around Christmas we filmed a banquet scene with six hundred costumed extras. We were by now months behind schedule and I had just sprained my back falling on some ice in front of the Eiffel Tower. The film negative went through the developing bath and came out with large white spots on the actors' faces. The final indignation occurred when I returned to the United States to find that my apartment, which I had not seen in eight months, had been gutted by a fire and flooded by a burst water pipe. All that was missing were locusts and the slaying of the firstborn."

The battle scenes were shot with real Russian soldiers. Woody was able to hire 1,000 Soviet troops as extras in Budapest. (The USSR Army is not one of the world's highest-paying employers . . .) They would, however, take orders only from their own officers. The translation problems, like Malthus' population projections, increased geometrically. Sometimes Woody's directions had to travel through four languages before they reached the Russian soldiers: from English to French to Hungarian to Russian. By then, the pre-set dynamite charges had already exploded and the entire process had to be repeated.

"It was not my idea of a good time," Woody said. "It worked . . . but at great expense to my emotional life."

Diane Keaton described the filming of *Love and Death* as "isolated. Only three people spoke English: Woody, his secretary, and myself. We didn't have much to say, so we'd sit in a trailer and talk in between shots, which took forever... And every day we would have the exact same meal in the hotel. Woody would have fish, and I would have chicken, no wine. The waiter thought we were the two most eccentric people in town."

Although close friends of Woody Allen and Diane Keaton knew their love affair had been over for several years, the movie-going public still thought of Diane Keaton as Woody Allen's girl friend. Not until June, 1975, when *Love and Death* was released, did news of their split appear in print.

A New York columnist said to Diane, "People keep asking me, 'Are Diane and Woody married?' "

"They do?" Diane said, wide-eyed. "I'll be darned." She thought about it a moment. "We aren't. Never were."

"You his 'lady' as they say nowadays?"

"No . . . Did we have a romance? Uh . . . we were . . . for awhile . . . a long time ago . . . years . . ."

At about the same time, Woody told a college press conference, "There's no romance between us. We haven't lived together in about four years."

Woody Allen and Diane Keaton, without public fanfare, made the rare transition from lovers to best friends. Nor, of course, did their professional relationship cease. Woody had long spoken of Keaton's "enormous talent."

* * * * * *

The spread of instant, electronic communication around the globe has reduced the gestation time for legends from several centuries to several years. The Beatles, for example, had become legends and stopped recording new albums before persons not keyed in to pop culture had a clear idea of just who they were.

Woody Allen continued to be astonished at the serious attention and the often tortured interpretations that were lavished on his movies. Once, after Woody lectured on his work at The New School for Social Research in New York, one young man insisted that *Love and Death* was obviously a carefully planned attack on the sexual mores of nineteenth century Russia. Woody found it hard to believe the young man was serious.

"Here I am just fighting for a laugh and trying to do a scene, and they're discussing it like it was genuinely Dostoevski," Woody said, awed. He was also becoming uncomfortable with the frequent critical comparisons between his movies and those of Charlie Chaplin and Buster Keaton.

"You can't compare," Woody insisted. "I'm working 40 years later. I'm a product of television and psychoanalysis. There's no similarity. I don't want my pictures to be compared with Keaton and Chaplin. It's tough being compared to old masters. What happens is you're a product of those comedians you liked. The same could be said of any other art form. If you look at many, many Picassos, you see Cezanne throughout."

Woody added that, however he was unconsciously influenced by Chaplin and Keaton, one of the most important conscious influences on his work was Bob Hope. "I don't like his politics, his television shows, but there was an enormous block of his work that included some fine movies that were flawed . . . I was very influenced by him. I have an enormous identity problem. I used to deliver like him. In fact, I feel I have characteristics in common with Hope. We're both cowards, womanizers, egotistical, vain. Hope was not a clown in the sense of Chaplin or Keaton. He was the guy next-door, the man from the electric company. You really believed him."

By this time in Woody's career, most critics agreed that he was the most important comic talent at work, certainly in the United States, possibly anywhere. But a number of them expressed doubts about the social value and ultimate artistic merit of Woody's movies. They could not accept the concept of comedy for its own sake which Woody advocated.

"I'm one of those people that believes that there's no social value in art—not just comedy, but no social value in art at all, anyplace. To me, all—opera, painting, anything—is a diversion, an entertainment. So I view my own work in that same way, that there is no social value. I don't think that it needs to be redeemed. I think it's strictly a pleasure item. If you have a certain set of values and a certain mentality, you get pleasure out of watching a situation comedy on television. And that's fine. Then someone else who has a more complex or, to me, a deeper grasp on life gets pleasure out of seeing a fine play or listening to a symphony. But in the end it's all entertainment. I don't believe in art as a social force."

* * * * * *

That summer of 1975 also saw the publication of Woody's second book, *Without Feathers*. Well over half the slim volume was taken up by two previously unpublished and unperformed one-act plays: *Death* and *God*. If these are one-acts that Woody had thought of bringing to Broadway, he's lucky that, for whatever reason, they never made it. His reputation would surely have suffered.

Neither *Death* nor *God* is as funny or as well-constructed as the much briefer *Death Knocks* (remember Nat Ackerman playing gin rummy with Death?) in his earlier book, *Getting Even*.

The title, *Without Feathers*, was derived from a line in an Emily Dickenson poem: "Hope is the thing with feathers." Woody, however, believes the belle of Amherst to be mistaken . . .

"How wrong Emily Dickinson was! Hope is not 'the thing with feathers.' The thing with feathers has turned out to be my nephew. I must take him to a specialist in Zurich."

Most of the comic essays in *Without Feathers* appeared first in either *The New Yorker* or *The New Republic*. Among Woody's targets this time around were:

Writer's diaries: *"Do I believe in God? I did until Mother's accident. She fell on some meat loaf, and it penetrated her spleen. She lay in coma for months, unable to do anything but sing 'Granada' to an imaginary herring. Why was this woman in the prime of life so afflicted—because in her youth she dared to defy convention and got married with a brown bag on her head? And how can I believe in God when just last week I got my tongue caught in the roller of an electric typewriter? I am plagued by doubts. What if everything is illusion and nothing exists? In that case, I definitely overpaid for my carpet. If only God would give me some clear sign! Like making a large deposit in my name at a Swiss bank."*

Biblical archeology: *"Scholars will recall that several years ago a shepherd, wandering in the Gulf of Aqaba, stumbled upon a cave containing several large clay jars and also two tickets to the ice show. Inside the jars were discovered six parchment scrolls with ancient incomprehensible writing which the shepherd, in his ignorance, sold to the museum for $750,000 apiece. . .The authenticity of the scrolls is currently in great doubt, particularly since the word 'Oldsmobile' appears several times in the text."*

Brooding Scandinavian playwrights: *(The character of) Mrs. Sanstad was Lovborg's revenge on his mother. Also a critical woman, she began life as a trapeze artist with the circus; his father, Nils Lovborg, was the human cannonball. The two met in midair and were married before touching ground. Bitterness slowly crept into the marriage, and by the time Lovborg was six years old his parents exchanged gunfire daily. This atmosphere took its toll on a sensitive youngster like Jorgen, and soon he began to suffer the first of his famous 'moods' and 'anxieties', rendering him for some years unable to pass a roast chicken without tipping his hat."*

The Dashiell Hammett-Raymond Chandler detectives (again): (Woody's protagonist, Kaiser Lupowitz, has just uncovered a ring of college call girls operating out of the Hunter College Book Store. They're selling their . . . minds.) *"But it wasn't just intellectual experiences—they were peddling emotional ones, too. For fifty bucks, I learned, you could 'relate without getting close'. For a hundred, a girl would lend you her Bartok records, have dinner, and then let you watch while she had an anxiety attack. For one-fifty, you could listen to FM radio with twins. For three bills, you got the works: A thin Jewish brunette would pretend to pick you up at the Museum of Modern Art, let you read her master's, get you involved in a screaming quarrel at Elaine's over Freud's conception of women, and then fake a suicide of your choosing—the perfect evening, for some guys. Nice racket. Great town, New York."*

* * * * * *

And finally—it was a busy summer—there was Woody's much-publicized "date" with Betty Ford. Newspapers all over the country ran photos of Woody Allen, in black tie and sneakers, escorting Mrs. Ford to a benefit performance for Martha Graham's dance company. Which, of course, was the precise purpose of the "date" which had been dreamed up by Tom Kerrigan, press aide to Ms. Graham.

Once you thought of it, the idea was a natural. After all, Woody Allen and Betty Ford were both former Graham students. Mrs. Ford had studied with Ms. Graham in the Thirties when the President's wife was still Elizabeth Bloomer. Woody's stint as a Graham student was more recent. A long-time admirer of Martha Graham's work, he had sweated through the beginner's class in the fall of 1974 so that he could "gain more insight into her work".

"I cramped every time," he added.

Woody said that he had written the first draft of a film script, *Dreams and Furies*, heavily influenced by Martha Graham's exploration of the hidden connections between psyche, myth and dramatic movement. Woody and Diane had attended all performances in the Graham company's 1974 season. "She's one of the few things that can get me out of the house," Woody said. "Graham is the other side of the comic prism, of the comic perspective."

Woody added that dancer/choreographer Martha Graham and film director Ingmar Bergman were the two artists who had most profoundly affected him. "So much of Graham's and Bergman's best works express the psychology of women. There are a lot of similarities.

"Graham is overpowering. The movements are so primordial that they're terrifying and irresistible. I'm much more partial to her darker pieces—*Clytemnestra, Night Journey*. I just prefer all that blood lust. She contacts me on the immediate level. I can only liken it to Bergman.

"The first time I saw Bergman's work, it was not something I was understanding intellectually. But it was totally compelling. I was on the edge of my seat. That can happen with Martha Graham. Bergman and she do the same exact thing. Both are very romantic in a certain sense, and both do highly theatrical things that are melodramatic but they come off as art.

"Both affect you in the same way. There is something terrifying about them. They create an atmosphere. They are two artists who have created their own vocabulary for expressing their personal obsessions."

Woody compared the absence of words in a Graham dance and a silent film comedy. He felt this silence gave both forms more power. "I'm at a disadvantage in making comic films," he said. "The appeal of the silent comedians was in the direct nonverbalness." He observed that Martha Graham also works "in this nonverbal primary way. She is the exact other side of the big laugh. Instead of a loud laugh, she goes for an equal response. She is not dealing with an intermediate area of pleasance. But like Bergman, she is a great entertainer."

Woody Allen displays the photographs of four women in his apartment: Louise Lasser, Diane Keaton, Liv Ullman and Martha Graham. These, he said, are the women he most respects and admires and, in Ms. Graham's case, idolizes. "I'm still at that adolescent stage of life—all that heroine and hero worship."

When Woody realized that he was finally going to meet

idol Graham the night of the benefit, he was, for a moment, panicked. "Martha Graham is one of those people I have not wanted to meet because I'd just as soon admire her from afar for the rest of our lives."

On June 19, 1975, the sidewalks in front of the Uris Theatre on West 51 Street were packed with security men, dance fans and celebrity watchers, in spite of the heavy rain. The Graham benefit had turned into *the* social event of the year and was drawing the sparkliest celebrities in New York. Paul Newman, Joanne Woodward and Lauren Bacall had already entered the lobby when Woody and Diane's limousine pulled up in front of the theatre. A few minutes later, Betty Ford, dressed in a purple chiffon gown, arrived, also by limousine.

As dozens of cameras clicked away, Woody walked beside Mrs. Ford into the theatre, with Diane just far enough away so she could be easily cropped out of the pictures. The White House and the Graham staff had also arranged for Mrs. Ford, Woody and Diane to be seated together.

At the first intermission, Woody joined Martha Graham and Betty Ford at a microphone set up in front of the Uris' red curtain. Ms. Graham and her former pupils spoke briefly to the audience.

"I'm a little overwhelmed," Martha Graham said. "I've never had such an array of cameras and such glamour treatment in my life. Even if this is just Cinderella for a night."

Then reporters were allowed to ask questions. They were most interested in Woody's relationship with Betty Ford.

"Why are you escorting Mrs. Ford?"

"We're just good friends," Woody said, in a deadpan parody of the standard brush-off that celebrities give gossip reporters when asked about a blossoming romance. Mrs. Ford smiled good-naturedly.

"Woody, why the sneakers?"

"I'm wearing sneakers because I think they look much nicer than the black shoes usually worn."

Asked about his impressions of Ms. Graham, Woody said, "I'm slightly uncomfortable around genius that is greater than my own."

The highlight of the evening, however, was its finale: Rudolf Nureyev and Margot Fonteyn in a new dance by Ms.

Graham called *Lucifer*. Graham made it clear she was not referring only to Satan. "Lucifer is also the god of light," she explained.

The evening was a grand success in every way, including the crucial financial one. The benefit earned $200,000 and made the Martha Graham troupe solvent for the first time in years. Woody's contribution was $5,000.

* * * * * *

On December 1, 1975, Woody Allen, the Eternal Adolescent, turned 40. In a birthday interview with Mel Gussow of *The New York Times*, Woody refused to see his fortieth birthday as any sort of milestone. 1975 was also the 200th anniversary of the U.S. Marine Corps which the *Times* said "has a great past, a troubled present and an uncertain future."

Woody saw certain similarities to his position in the world. "I have a troubled past, a troubled present and a troubled future.

"I'm becoming more attractive with age," he said, brightening. "I'm getting to look less like a punk. I want to be leading-man age. I think I'll be gorgeous at 50. I think that's a nice age for women—and for women."

Woody said he did not plan to ever get a facelift. "I don't even have my teeth filled."

He said that he had given up his dreams of Brigitte Bardot and of being a professional athlete. "I'll never show up at baseball spring training or at the Knicks' training camp . . . We are all taught to value the mind over the body. Just the opposite should be true. Achievements of the mind are full of complexities and self-delusions. When we see athletes do something perfect, it's very pure and genuine. You can't fool The Body."

Woody offered numerous pithy one-liners on his fortieth birthday, most of them on his favorite subjects of love and death.

On Love: "*. . . bisexuality . . . immediately doubles your chances for a date on Saturday night.*"

"*Love is the answer. But while you're waiting for the answer, sex raises some pretty good questions.*"

On Psychoanalysis: *"When I first started going, I was worried my personality would be changed to conform to a norm representing a typical middle class Viennese of 1920. Now I'd be willing to settle for that."*

"It's hard to feel confidence in an analyst who doesn't wear a belt, showlaces or a tie." (Woody Allen's analyst is a woman.)

On Younger Women: *"I dated a 21-year-old girl. Took her to my apartment. Put on a record of Charlie Parker and Dizzy Gillespie playing a Cole Porter tune. She thought it was classical music."*

On Death: *"The difference between sex and death is, with death you can do it alone and nobody's going to make fun of you."*

Then Woody's birthday thoughts took a more serious turn: "The world is increasingly more sophisticated and complex. It takes an enormous amount of effort to keep informed. If I were doing comedy monologues now, I would have to be informed about politics, genetics, sociobiology, behavioral psychology."

The old theme of his wish to tackle more serious subjects arose once again. "I want to do more risky films, less conventional ones, films I'm not secure with. I only just learned how to make films. The first few times I was just noodling around. I'm going to aim higher, and I want to push the audience with me."

Woody reiterated his dislike of the "technical and boring" aspects of filmmaking as well as the huge time commitment necessary. "It means going into the deep freeze for at least a year. On my set there's no sense of community or intramural jocularity. I'm always cranky and complaining.

"(But) the impact of movies is so great, and in a certain way, it's so satisfying . . . Not to mention the girls!"

Woody's birthday interview took place during a break in the shooting of *The Front*, a film on the McCarthy era in which Woody was playing his first serious role. "I'm very curious to see if I have a flair for this. It wouldn't surprise me if I didn't."

chapter 7

A Change

of Direction

WOODY ALLEN HAS SAID that he grew up in Brooklyn largely unaware of political issues. "I seldom read newspapers, outside of the sports section. I had a general awareness of Joseph McCarthy—I remember the 5 o'clock shadow and that kind of villainous look—but I wasn't aware of the implications of McCarthyism at all. I recall that neighbors of mine in Flatbush went to a Paul Robeson concert and got stoned by a mob and had their car smashed. When I heard about that, I considered it for a minute and then I turned on the ball game."

Not until the early Sixties, nearly ten years later, did Woody begin to understand the full depth of what the McCarthy era was all about. He had an engagement at the hungry i in San Francisco. Running the lights was Alvah Bessie, a former Hollywood scriptwriter who could no longer work in the movie industry because he'd been blacklisted. "Once we were coming out of a restaurant and a man getting out of a car gave Alvah a cheerful hello," Woody recalls. "Alvah said, 'How can you say hello to me, after the things you said about me?' And then he punched the man. Moments later, I got a glimpse of how deep-rooted that feeling of acute bitterness is among those who were blacklisted."

The blacklist. The execution of the Rosenbergs. The persecution of Alger Hiss and the very real possibility that the FBI forged evidence against him. Today, it seems inconceivable that such madness could ever have seized the political life of the United States, land of the brave, home of the free. But it did.

Alvah Bessie's name had appeared on a list of alleged Communists and Communist sympathizers. Lists of this type were sent by various right-wing publications—Red Channels and Counterattack were two of most notorious—to the television and radio networks and all the Hollywood movie studios. The threat, especially powerful with television executives, was that dire economic and other reprisals would follow if persons on the lists were employed.

The lists were constructed capriciously, primarily from hearsay and rumor. American Communist Party members were, of course, listed, along with persons who had merely expressed a too-enthusiastic commitment to civil rights or had lent their names to a cause or event the list-makers found suspect. Guilt by association was rampant. For awhile it seemed the list-makers equated "outspoken liberal" with "Communist sympathizer". American artists and entertainers who were blacklisted include Leonard Bernstein, Lillian Hellman, Arthur Miller, Aaron Copland, Artie Shaw, Lena Horne and Gypsy Rose Lee. During much of the 1950's these men and women could not get work in radio, television or movies.

The blacklist didn't include just big names. Several hundred men and women were involved: writers, directors, musicians, composers, actors, actresses, most of them unknown to the general public.

Two of the lesser known names on the blacklist were Walter Bernstein and Martin Ritt. Bernstein wrote for both Hollywood and television in the late Forties. Among his screen credits are *All the King's Men* and *Kiss the Blood Off My Hands*. In June, 1950, Walter Bernstein found himself— courtesy of Red Channels—on the blacklist. He didn't work under his own name for eight years. Bernstein was lucky. As a writer, he could sell his work by using a "front", a person who, for ten per cent of the take, would present a blacklisted writer's work as his own.

Martin Ritt was not so lucky. As an actor, he could hardly have a "front". Blacklisted in 1951 for six years, Ritt kept his hand in by directing at Lee Strassberg's Actors Studio. In 1957, he was hired to direct a movie, *Edge of the City*, by

David Susskind who was quite deliberately testing the power of the blacklist. Ritt's career since then has been as director, not actor. His movies include *Hud* and *Sounder*.

The late Zero Mostel, after several successful years in the early Fifties as an actor in supporting roles at Twentieth Century Fox, was blacklisted. Unable to work in Hollywood, Mostel came to New York. There were several lean years before Mostel made a name for himself in the theatre with his portrait of Leopold Bloom in the Off-Broadway production of *Ulysses in Nighttown.* The Sixties were good years for Mostel. He had a string of Broadway hits, including *Rhinoceros, A Funny Thing Happened on the Way to the Forum* and the triumph of his career, *Fiddler on the Roof.*

In 1955, however, Mostel could hardly imagine such a bright future. He ended his testimony before the televised hearings of HUAC (House Committee on Un-American Activities) by saying, "I want to thank the Committee for making it possible for me to be on TV because I've been blacklisted for five years."

Mostel's reemergence on national TV after his long absence included several delicious, albeit bitter, bits of comedy.

"What studio were you with?" HUAC's chairman asked.

"Eighteenth Century Fox," Mostel earnestly replied.

"Do you want that statement to stand?" the chairman asked, vastly annoyed.

"No, make it Nineteenth Century Fox," Mostel said.

When he refused to answer questions, he raised his hand and wiggled his five fingers to indicate he was taking the Fifth Amendment.

* * * * * *

Walter Bernstein and Martin Ritt first met several years before the American Inquisition when Ritt appeared in a television show that Bernstein had written. When the blacklist era was over, they worked together on two films—*Paris Blues* in 1961 and *The Molly Maguires* in 1970.

During the filming in Pennsylvania of *The Molly Maguires*, Bernstein and Ritt spent many hours talking about doing a movie on the blacklist. But it was a difficult subject. The reality of those times was so terrible they couldn't see how to do a movie that wouldn't be top-heavy with preaching and finger-pointing. Finally, Bernstein realized that by telling a sometimes funny story about a "front", such as he himself had used during the time he was blacklisted, he could obliquely relate some very serious truths in a more light-hearted way.

Ritt agreed this was a good approach and Bernstein set to work writing a screenplay. After being turned down by several studios, Bernstein and Ritt made a deal with David Begelman, president of Columbia, whom Ritt said was willing "to stick out his neck and take a chance."

Woody Allen agreed to act in *The Front* even before Bernstein had begun writing the screenplay. "I was responsive to the material," he said. "It's a semi-serious comedy-drama about the blacklisting era. It's a shameful era and one that has never been explored."

In *The Front*, Woody Allen plays a restaurant cashier and two-bit Brooklyn bookie who becomes a front for a blacklisted television writer. Allen's cashier can hardly write a grocery list much less a television play, but soon he is a celebrity living in an elegant Manhattan apartment and loved by a beautiful young script editor played by Andrea Marcovicci.

"I decided to take a chance," Woody said. "From the beginning, I had enormous reservations about doing a film which I had not written and over which I would have no directorial control. I wasn't sure how I would feel being a hired actor in a dramatic movie, and I said, 'If you want a guy to make *conversation*, hire Jack Nicholson.'

"I felt uncomfortable throughout the whole process, not being able to improvise and change things. And I could never judge how things were going. My only yardstick is funniness. I can look at the dailies on one of my own movies, and maybe I don't look too attractive up on that screen or maybe I don't move so gracefully, but I just *know* when it's funny, and I know immediately when something is missing. But when I look at the dailies on a dramatic film, I'm all at sea."

"I don't think *The Front* is an angry movie. It is not a devastating indictment of the blacklist. I believe it is meant to be an entertaining reminder that these things went on in this country in 1953, that people were losing jobs, committing suicide, and other people were behaving, *choosing* to behave, in terrible ways. What would have been truly courageous would have been to make the film in 1953, but of course Marty Ritt and Walter Bernstein couldn't get a job in Hollywood then. Now it's an utterly, utterly safe project, conceivably one that studios see a buck in from the entertainment point of view."

Just how safe the blacklist and the McCarthy Era had become can be seen in the response that Ritt received when he queried the television networks about whether they would be interested in buying broadcast rights. All three networks said that yes, they would definitely be interested. A CBS memo is especially illustrative of the changed atmosphere: "We particularly like it because it deals with a subject that is now comfortably historical."

Bernstein had written a part for Zero Mostel based in large part on Zero's own experiences during the blacklist. Mostel had been a nightclub comedian before he had turned to acting, just like his character in *The Front*.

In the movie, Mostel, desperate for work, gets a job at a Catskills resort only to find out when he arrives that the owner has drastically cut the fee they'd agreed on earlier. Mostel's desperation and grief explode into a destructive rage that nearly consumes him.

What happened in real life wasn't too different from the way Bernstein presents it. In his book, *A Journal of the Plague Years*, Stefan Kanfer describes the incident: "In 1958, the needy Zero Mostel agreed to do a club date in the Catskills. He had intended to trot out his *schticks* from the days of the *boites*. But when he arrived at the resort, he found that the manager had reduced the rate from $300 to $150. Raging, emptying tumblers of Scotch, Mostel eventually reeled onstage and delivered his entire act in Yiddish, pouring torrents of abuse upon his audience. With transcendent obtuseness, his audience applauded enthusiastically; they had interpreted the routine as insult comedy."

A far more tragic real life connection is contained within *The Front*'s plot. Toward the end of the film, the Mostel character commits suicide by jumping from a hotel window. In 1955, a talented actor named Philip Loeb killed himself with an overdose of sleeping pills at Manhattan's Hotel Taft.

Broke and desperate, Loeb had been living at Zero Mostel's apartment on West 86th Street. Once Papa Goldberg on the popular television series, *The Goldbergs*,

Loeb had been a prime target for the blacklisters: In 1936, he had signed a defense of the Moscow Trials in the magazine, *New Masses*. But if political naivete always meant lifetime unemployment, how many of us could keep our jobs?

* * * * * *

The Front was filmed in Manhattan during the late fall and early winter of 1975. Bernstein and Ritt were apprehensive that publicity about Zero Mostel and Woody Allen doing a movie together was bound to be misunderstood.

"The point to be stressed about *The Front*," Bernstein said, "is that while it has a good deal of comedy in it—or at least I hope so—it is basically a very serious movie, a morality tale. Audiences expecting to see Mostel as he was in *The Producers* or Woody Allen as he was in *Sleeper* or *Love and Death* are going to be sorely disappointed in *The Front*. Zero's part is serious and highly emotional. And Woody plays what amounts to a straight part—he does no comic *shtick* and has no gag lines. I guess what I've written is a serious comedy."

Ritt pointed out that *The Front* was bitterly relevant to much recent U.S. history. "After all, the blacklist paved the way to things like Nixon's enemies list and secret F.B.I. files on political dissenters. And the anti-Communist hysteria of the 1950's paved the way, in my opinion, to Vietnam and to the political climate that led to Watergate."

Ritt said that the practice of blacklisted writers using fronts "personified the hypocrisy of the blacklist, because it must be remembered that the TV networks and movie studios were fully aware of the fact that they were dealing with blacklisted writers through fronts. In fact, they were delighted to accept scripts from fronts, because the fronts were ostensibly unknown beginners who couldn't command the high price per script that more established writers got. The ugly truth is that there was never any morality or even anti-Communist feeling involved in the attitude of the networks toward those of us who'd been blacklisted. They didn't hire us for economic reasons—that is, they were afraid that they'd lose sponsors if they overtly used blacklisted writers or performers. In a way, the blacklist was hilarious but, on the other hand, it was really far from funny.

"Children of blacklisted actors were jeered at in school as 'Red Commie bastards', marriages broke up, careers were wrecked, financial ruin fell upon many, and I know of at least one black-listed performer who committed suicide because he was dead broke and unable to find work. A few of us came through the experience of being blacklisted relatively unhurt—we're the lucky ones."

Woody Allen expressed ambivalence on the question of whether the blacklist or something comparable could happen again. "Our government has disgraced itself so consistently that the general public wouldn't let it happen again. If it *does* happen again, it will happen in some new and more sophisticated manner."

Woody also said that his work in the Bernstein-Ritt project did not represent a permanent change of direction in his career. "I have no yen to be a dramatic actor. I didn't look at *The Front* as my chance to play *Hamlet*. If they had offered me Ratso Rizzo in *Midnight Cowboy* or *Serpico*, I don't think I would have said yes. Although the role in *The Front* was on another level from what I've done before, it wasn't on another planet. I didn't prepare it any special way. I wouldn't know where to begin to prepare.

"In truth, no responsible person in the movie industry ever offered me a serious role before, though occasionally somebody will send me a preposterous script, either a crazy, surreal thing about spiders taking over the world, or a dirty story about a sex clinic. The reason I did *The Front* was that the *subject* was worthwhile. Martin Ritt and Walter Bernstein lived through the blacklist and survived it with dignity, so I didn't mind deferring to their judgment.

". . . I read it and thought how nice it would be to act, for a change, in something where I didn't constantly have to go for the gags. It's that simple. I have no ambitions to go on being a 'serious' actor.

"And I could relax," Woody continued, "in the sense that, no matter what happened, my script couldn't get mangled. It *wasn't* my script."

* * * * * *

As soon as Ritt completed the filming of *The Front* early in 1976, Woody Allen began the pre-production work for his next movie. The idea for it had been in his mind since *Sleeper*, along with several others that were far more developed. He thought he would begin fliming one of the latter in June, 1974. That's not the way it worked out.

"I wanted to do a deeper comedy," Woody said. "I wanted to do a more human film—a comedy but a real person. Not a guy wakes up in the future, or a guy is a bank robber, or a guy takes over a Latin American country. I wanted to do one where I play me, Diane plays her, we live in New York. Conflict but real, as opposed to too flamboyant an idea . . . I don't know if I'm doing the right thing or not in the sense that I might write a real story and people will come and they'll laugh at it but I'll get the same kind of reactions in certain quarters that I got with *Sam*: 'Yeah, I expected more far-out stuff, more imaginative stuff; whereas the thing I'm working on fits right into the type of film people expect of me."

So Woody temporarily shelved the movie in which he and Diane Keaton would play themselves and made *Love and Death* instead. Another inevitable delay occurred for the filming of *The Front*. When that commitment was fulfilled, Woody Allen was ready, both professionally and emotionally, to begin making what he called his first serious comedy.

"I've always been able to get laughs," he said. "I wanted to move on. This is not a quantum leap, but at least it's a couple of inches in the right direction . . . I think people will say that my new film is different by light years from anything I've ever done. The style of film is different, my character is different. It's another romantic comedy like *Sam* but it's much more serious. *Sam* was a trivial, amusing thing. I think people will take more away from this one on deeper levels."

Filming began on Monday, May 10, 1976 on Long Island's South Fork. Possibly unsure of what would happen once he left behind his old policy of sacrificing everything for the laugh, Woody insisted on total and complete secrecy. The only thing his office would say was that the new movie was a romantic comedy, starred Woody and Diane Keaton and that other scenes in the movie would be shot in Brooklyn and Manhattan.

"Mr. Allen is totally involved in the film and doesn't want publicity," a spokesman said. Which, of course, is a statement guaranteed to generate publicity.

For months, the only information that Woody would give about his new movie was "It's a contemporary, loosely auto-biographical romantic comedy with myself, Diane Keaton, Shelly Duvall, Colleen Dewhurst and Paul Simon."

The speculation increased right along with the secrecy. Woody and a film crew had been spotted at the rollercoaster on Coney Island. Someone else discovered that many scenes had been shot in the apartment of Richard Runes, a lawyer who lived in the Hotel des Artistes near Lincoln Center. Woody and Diane were filmed eating lunch at a restaurant across the street from the New York State Theater at Lincoln Center.

But no details were forthcoming from either the United Artists publicity department or from Woody Allen. The movie didn't even have a name. Its working title, as far as Woody and co-writer Marshall Brickman were concerned, was *Anhedonia*. But Woody and Marshall finally agreed that, since probably only one out of every one hundred people knew what "anhedonia" was, they would be better off finding another title. When they got the news, there were no doubt dozens of immensely relieved United Artists executives. *Anhedonia* is a title that does not immediately suggest huge box-office potential.

"Anhedonia is a psychological state where nothing gives a person pleasure," Woody explained. "The word hedonism is in it. We diagnosed that as Alvy's problem; nothing gives him any pleasure." (Ah ha! So there is a character named Alvy.. .)

"I think everyone suffers from it," Woody declared, "just as everyone is a little paranoid. I don't develop big enthusiasms. I find filmmaking laborious and tedious. I try to mitigate it by working with Diane, who I like a lot. This time I have myself a very big treat by working in New York. I think I will try to make all my films here."

By the end of the year, the film was in the can, but there was still no title. United Artists ads in the trades simply referred to "the new Woody Allen movie". Woody and Marshall continued to dream up titles and Woody set to work with Ralph Rosenblum on the huge editing task.

As usual, Woody had shot more than 100,000 feet of film. He and Rosenblum would have to cut about 50 *hours* of film down to about ninety minutes.

"I love annihilating film when we're cutting it," Woody

says. "Getting it down from a hundred and twenty-four minutes to eighty-nine. I think eight-nine minutes may be the perfect length for something funny, don't you?"

Woody and Rosenblum needed about four months to edit "the new Woody Allen movie." All Rosenblum would say about his current assignment was, "It's terribly funny. It's more personal, more heavily plotted than anything he's done. For me it's his best film."

Woody says he and his film editor spend much of their time arguing. "He'd say, 'Gee, I think you're much funnier in take two of that scene.' I'd say, 'Yeah, but Keaton's better in take three.' I want an atmosphere, on any picture of mine, where I can be disagreed with."

There was little time to spare. "The new Woody Allen movie" was to premiere at Filmex, the Los Angeles Film Exposition, on March 27, 1977. Editing of the film was completed less than a month before the release date. Only three weeks before the premiere did Woody Allen decide on a name for his sixth feature film.

He decided he would call the new movie *Annie Hall*.

After the Los Angeles premiere but before the New York release date in late April, Woody described for the first time what Annie Hall was all about.

"The story revolves around a guy of about 40—I'm 42—who's re-examining his whole life, and his relationships with women, particularly this one relationship with one girl, and why it hasn't worked out as they'd both hoped. Well, Diane Keaton, who's been in four of my pictures, is the most important relationship in *my* life. And Diane plays Annie Hall. And in that sense, the movie's loosely autobiographical . . .

"I wanted it to be about . . . us, *real* people, *real* problems besetting some fairly neurotic characters trying to exist in male-female relationships in America in 1977. So it turns out to be more serious than anything I've ever tried before."

In *Annie Hall*, Woody said, "I play a comedian. Diane sings, I'm friends with Tony Roberts and almost everybody I know has moved out to California. I was not married to a New York intellectual nor to anyone particularly committed—as in the movie. I lived with Diane for a year when we were doing *Play It Again, Sam* on Broadway, but we're still the best of friends."

Woody Allen and Marshall Brickman had striven to produce a script that was both comic and Bergmanesque: "a stream of consciousness showing one individual's state of mind, in which conversations and events constantly trigger dreams, fantasies and recollections."

Brickman still wouldn't say which lines in *Annie Hall* were his and which were Woody's. He was more interested in the problems they faced as writers, rather than in the details of the collaboration.

"At first, we made Diane Keaton a neurotic New York girl," Brickman said, "but the character had no dramatic transition. This led us to giving her a family in Wisconsin. You keep asking each other—who is this guy, what are his values? Face it, the movie only hints at profound issues, but we asked ourselves, 'Is it neurosis or honesty that makes the character Woody plays so pessimistic? Is it merely maladjustment, immaturity, or is it a relentless philosophical integrity?' "

Woody believes these kinds of concerns are one of the reasons *Annie Hall* is such a departure from his previous work. "*Annie's* a big step forward, *miles* from the slapstick of, say *Bananas* . . . I think of the movie as a *romantic* comedy . . . Okay, gentle, then. It *is* a comedy. It's just not my usual."

Finally, *Annie Hall* opened in New York. There were lines two blocks long for most screenings. Weekends were impossible. One of the reasons for the crush was that people were going back a second, a third time to see *Annie Hall*.

It is early in the film. Alvy Singer (Woody Allen) and Annie Hall (Diane Keaton) have just met on the tennis court. Now they've showered and dressed and they run into each other in the lobby of the Manhattan tennis club where they've played. Alvy's clothes are serviceable and nondescript. But Annie? Annie is wearing baggy tan men's trousers, a white men's shirt, a black tie (men's, of course) with white polka dots and a black vest. Her hair has been mostly captured under an impossible black hat (a rabbi's?) of indeterminate age and gender.

"*Hi! Hi!*" She says to Alvy. She looks at him expectantly. She smiles, eyes wide. Alvy is still trying to deal with her outfit. When he doesn't speak, Annie waves again, "*Well . . . bye!*" and turns toward the door. Alvy springs into action.

"*You play very well,*" he says.

"*Oh, yeah? So do you!*" Annie says expansively. Then her face falls. She's done it again.

"*Oh, god, oh . . . what a dumb thing to say, right? You*

say, 'You play well,' then right away I have to say, 'You play well.' " She puts her hands on her hips as if she has suddenly become the exasperated mother to the small girl in herself. She shakes her head. What *is* she going to do with this wayward brat? The small girl drops her hand from the maternal hip and raises it beseechingly. *"Oh, god, Annie . . . well, oh, well . . ."* Tomorrow is, after all, another day: *"La-dee-dah . . . la-dee-dah."*

She shrugs and turns again to leave. Alvy offers her a ride. She accepts. Then she remembers her own car is outside. Alvy is increasingly confused. What does she mean?

"Ah, I don't—I, jeez, I don't know, I wasn't . . ." Annie would love to know what she's doing. She jerks her hand to the door. *"You know, I have a car. Why didn't I remember that?"* She sighs. *"I got this VW out there."* Alvy is speechless. He just stares. Annie feels herself sinking into a morass of missed meanings.

"What a jerk," she says, looking at the floor as if there were a mirror in it.

Finally, she shrugs, giving up on the whole impossible task of making a good impression. She laughs. *"Would you like a lift?"*

Who could say no? Although after he finds out the way Annie drives—erratic but fast is a kind of description of her performance behind the wheel—Alvy may have wished he had taken the subway home.

Annie has other idiosyncracies—at least to Alvy: an inability to engage in sex without the help of marijuana, spiders in her bathroom and a very typical middle-American family in Chippewa Falls, Wisconsin, all of which Annie Hall deals with in its ninety minutes. Diane Keaton wanted it understood that *Annie Hall* was not literal, verbatim-type truth: "It's not true, but there are *elements* of truth in it," Keaton said. "It's about a relationship, and because Woody and I know each other well and have had a relationship, there's a quality of truth in it. My real last name is Hall, for instance.

"But we didn't meet on the tennis court; we met at an audition for Woody's play, *Play It Again, Sam.* I have a Volkswagen, but I'm a *slow* driver, a cautious driver, too slow. I'm a nervous wreck when I meet a man, but I don't smoke marijuana at all. I have in the past, when I was in *Hair.* But it makes me a little nervous, and I feel nervous enough without it. I like a glass of wine, which makes me more relaxed. My parents are not from Wisconsin, but Balboa Island, California, and they're nothing at all like the parents in the film—but they are *goyim*. I've never had spiders in my bathtub. Roaches, maybe."

So *there*.

Woody frequently returns to the childhood past of Alvy Singer who grew up in a house under the Coney Island roller coaster. In the summer, every time the cars hurtle past, the house shakes as if an earthquake is in progress. Woody had originally intended to film the childhood scenes at his own birthplace on Avenue K in Brooklyn. But one day he was out scouting other locations with his art director and he spotted the house under the roller coaster. Woody knew exactly what he was going to do.

"I want to get that house," he told the art director.

He also changed the script, making Alvy's father the man who runs the bumper-car concession at Coney Island rather than a taxi-driver as originally planned.

"There's one clear autobiographical fact in the picture," Woody said. "I've thought about sex since my first intimation of consciousness." One of the scenes in *Annie Hall* that is clearly derived from the work of Ingmar Bergman is when Alvy, now grown up, visits his childhood self in the classroom as the character in *Wild Strawberries* did.

Alvy is a precocious child. In addition to sex, he frets from an early age about the end of the universe which he has learned is expanding at a fantastic rate. One day it will have run down completely and then what?

"Why is that your business?" his distraught mother asks, her voice rising. *"Brooklyn is not expanding!"*

Alvy will not be consoled.

* * * * * *

The perilous drive from the tennis club is over. Annie has invited Alvy up to her apartment for a glass of wine. Now they are out on Annie's tiny terrace, leaning against its railing, sooty Manhattan buildings in the background. They're trying hard to impress each other with meaningless pseudo-intellectual babble. What they're thinking appears in titles on the bottom of the screen.

Annie: *He thinks I'm stupid.*

Alvy: *She thinks I'm a jerk.*

Finally, Annie decides to get down to basics. She will immediately put into practice that ancient female wisdom that decrees: Let's talk about *you!*

"Well, now, you're what Grammy Hall would call a 'real Jew'. She hates Jews. She thinks they just make money, but let me tell you, she's the one, is she ever."

Which induces in Alvy one of the funniest "takes" in the history of cinema.

Yes, there is a Grammy Hall, alive and well in California. Now in her eighties, Grammy Hall thought *Annie Hall* a very funny movie. "That Woody Allen," Grammy Hall says, "he's something! I can't make head or tail out of half of what he says."

For his part, Woody Allen found Grammy Hall a rare bird. "I remember having Thanksgiving dinner at one of her grammy's houses. A beautiful American family. I felt I was an alien or exotic object to them, a nervous, anxiety-ridden, suspicious, wise-cracking kind of strange bird. Actually, that wasn't so far off from what it was. After dinner, all these Grammys sat around playing penny poker. I couldn't believe it. My family would have been exchanging gunfire."

There were other culture shocks for New Yorker Woody Allen. One time he and Diane were visiting her parents in California. Diane needed some chewing gum. A supermarket was less than half a block away.

"Well, let's get in the car and go," Diane said, keys already in her hand.

"You're going to get in the car and go?" Woody said, amazed that Diane could even think about getting in a car in order to drive less than 400 feet.

"You're not going to walk, are you?" Diane said. Now she was the amazed one.

"Well, yeah, of course, I mean, I walk *30 times* that length without thinking to get the newspapers."

Diane could hardly believe this, at least as Woody Allen tells the story. But she deferred to his wishes—after all, Woody was her guest—and discovered that it was indeed possible to walk to the supermarket.

"You know, hey, I guess you *can* walk!" Diane said.

* * * * * *

In *Annie Hall*, Alvy and Annie conduct their sex life not only in bed, but on their respective analysts' couches.

"How often do you have sex?" asks Alvy's shrink, a fatherly type.

"Hardly ever," answers Alvy, grieving. *"Maybe three times a week."*

Now the dialogue shifts to the other side of the split screen. *"How often do you have sex?"* asks Annie's shrink, a motherly type.

"All the time," Annie says, overwhelmed. *"At least three times a week."*

We live in times that are not conducive to enduring male-female relationships and Woody Allen, in this scene, illustrates one of the reasons why. Given the same set of facts, men and women place them in totally different emotional contexts. It never occurs to Alvy to explore Annie's emotional landscape. All his energies are spent trying to make her agree that his emotional values are the right ones. Alvy would never dream of trying to find out why Annie cannot respond whole-heartedly to his lovemaking. That would mean risking his version of *macho*: the Jewish male's need for total and complete belief in his own intellectual superiority.

Early in the movie, on Alvy's first visit to Annie's apartment, this interchange takes place:

Alvy picks up a book. *"Sylvia Plath. An interesting poetess whose tragic suicide was misinterpreted as romantic by the college-girl mentality."*

"Oh; yeah, right," Annie says, then has second thoughts. *"I don't know, some of her poems seemed neat to me."*

" 'Neat?' I hate to tell you this, but it's 1975. 'Neat' went out about the turn of the century."

Now, if Annie had tried to impress Alvy by this type of not-terribly-subtle intellectual put-down, he would not have found it even slightly appealing. Why on earth does he imagine that Annie will be smitten by such behavior on his part?

Not that Annie (or most any woman) would become con-sciously angry over such insulting behavior. Most women, from the cradle, are encouraged to defer to the intellectual superiority of men. But the resentment at having to pretend that such a patent absurdity is true goes underground and is transformed into sexual reluctance or worse, a total lack of sexual response, at least to the male. (Most so-called non-orgasmic women have no trouble reaching orgasm via masturbation.)

The only strategy that Alvy can think of to improve their sex life is to buy a red light bulb. For all his vaunted intellectual prowess, not to mention his voracious sexual appetite, Alvy shows a curious lack of imagination when it comes to making love.

Diane Keaton declines to say whether Woody Allen was as hilarious a lover as he is a comic. She approves, however, of "amusing things" occasionally happening in bed: "I don't want to have anything to do with someone who can't make fun of it once in a while."

Keaton's view of *Annie Hall* is, not surprisingly, remarkably similar to Woody Allen's. She says the movie is about "how difficult it is for two sort of neurotic people who like each other to have a relationship in New York and keep it going. I think Woody's saying something about the fact that it is very difficult nowadays to have a romance, especially when you're single and ambitious, and have nothing to hold on to, like a family. Things have changed a lot since birth control and the women's movement, and there's no emphasis now on God. Relationships are very difficult, especially for someone like me, who's 31, ambitious and single and lives in New York."

Diane Keaton lives on East 68th Street in Manhattan in a sparsely furnished, mostly white apartment with two bedrooms, one of which she has converted to a darkroom. Photography is a serious pursuit of Keaton's (a six-page spread of her work has appeared in *Photoworld* magazine) and she's fond of doing geometric line drawings and making collages from newspaper and magazine clips. She says that while making *Annie Hall* she and Woody sometimes felt an acute sense of emotional embarrassment. They were, after all, dealing with their own lives.

"It's always embarrassing to reveal my personal life," Diane says, "but emotional embarrassment is a condition of acting. (You are) revealing yourself even when you're not playing your own life. The biggest worry I had making *Annie Hall* was whether or not I would get in my own way. I was afraid that unconsciously I might stop myself from showing the truth because it made me uncomfortable ... But the whole process of acting is uncomfortable anyway.

"I wanted to do *Annie Hall* fully, without worrying what I did wrong in real life. Understand? I had to stop fantasizing about what kind of person I am. Am I bad? Was I wrong in that situation? Did I hurt Woody too much? Was I selfish? There were so many conflicts . . . But in the final analysis, working out my relationship with Woody was, and still is, great fun, and always a surprise and a revelation to me."

Diane Keaton does not like it one bit when reporters imply that without Woody Allen she would have had no career at all. "I wouldn't say that," she says, her voice suddenly hard and icy. "Things in life happen. I hope there would be a way for me to work without having met him. I'd have to say that I think I'd be able to work without him.

"I feel that everybody has a career based on somebody and we're influenced by somebody, and I have to feel that I have the talent to back it up. And I feel I've worked hard. I don't agree with that. Otherwise, I'd kill myself."

Woody Allen says, gallantly and no doubt truthfully, that Keaton has been of enormous help to *his* career. "I have not been a crutch for her at all. It's been absolutely aboveboard. You could reverse that and think that she's been a crutch to me in many ways. I mean, she's been an enormously supportive person to *me* on projects.

"(She's) the best person in the world to let read a script, because she's totally ingenuous. She's not trying to be impressive, she doesn't care if it was written by Chekhov. She's perfectly willing to pick it up, read it and say, 'I think it's boring' or 'I think it's wonderful.' I feel secure working with her. If she tells me something is creepy, I re-examine it.

"Diane was just born funny," Woody continues. "She can take a perfectly straight paragraph and read it and you'll be rolling on the floor. She has unfailing good taste. Her mind is never clouded by popular opinion, the need to score points. I can show her something and say the two greatest writers in the world love it, and she can pick it up and say 'I don't know what's so great about this.' And she'll be right."

Similarly, Diane Keaton has nothing but good things to say about Woody Allen. "I'm comfortable with him. We're very good friends. I talk to him a lot, and we see each other every week. We laugh and share things. He's very good to his friends, he's always been tremendously encouraging to them, always giving them a big push.

"Woody and I . . . we're beyond getting involved again

with each other ... and beyond really hurting each other,
which is a wonderful place to get with someone you love ...
there's humor, affection, and a certain dependency between
us. He's my closest and dearest friend."

Two people who were obviously made for each other... so
why did Woody Allen and Diane Keaton, Alvy Singer and
Annie Hall, split up?

In the movie, Annie wants to get out more, meet more
people. After her singing debut in a small nightclub, a record
promoter (Paul Simon) invites her and Alvy to a party. Annie
wants to go; Alvy doesn't: they don't go.

"You're an island unto yourself, like New York City,"
Annie says. *"You're incapable of enjoying life."*

Annie moves to California to pursue her singing career
and stays with the record promoter. Packing her books in
Alvy's apartment, she observes that all the books he gave her
have "death" in the title. Alvy follows her to California and
asks her to marry him. She says no.

Months later, Alvy is still trying to figure it out: *"Annie
and I broke up and I still can't get my mind around that, you
know, I keep sifting the pieces of the relationship through my
mind and examining my life and trying to figure out where the
screw-up came."*

Woody Allen, however, declares that's not the way it happened. "It was nothing like that," he says. She was not involved with anybody else and she wasn't running away to
California. She lived here and at one point we talked about
the idea that we had been living so closely for years and it
might be nice, we thought, to try it with her *not* living here.
This was a mutual decision. And if we didn't like that, we'd
move back in together again. And she took an apartment, and
I helped her move in and all that, and we were very friendly
and still seeing each other. I mean, we were still lovers inter-
mittently after that for a while. Gradually, we sort of cooled
down and drifted apart more. But it was *nothing* like in the
movie."

Diane Keaton says she doesn't exactly *know* why she and
Woody split. "It's very hard to say."

* * * * * *

Technically, *Annie Hall*, Woody's sixth film, was a very
long way from his first effort, *Take the Money and Run*, a

raw and ragged movie that appeared to have been put together by high-school movie-making class. Very deliberately, Woody planned a three-color scheme for *Annie Hall* with photographer Gordon Willis. The scenes dealing with Annie and Alvy's love story were shot only on gray, overcast days or at sundown, "the most romantic light". Scenes dealing with Alvy's childhood are artificially filtered to come out "very yellow and golden," which Woody says is the color of nostalgia. The California scenes—and Woody makes no bones about hating California—are shot "right into the sun. Everybody is so white they seem to vaporize."

Financially, *Annie Hall* was a solid hit. By mid-summer, 1977, it had grossed $25 million. The movie enjoyed smashing critical success as well. All the major U.S. movie critics unashamedly adored *Annie Hall*; they felt the movie was a major artistic breakthrough for Woody Allen.

New York Times movie critic Vincent Canby, always an enthusiastic admirer of Woody'w work, was totally carried away by *Annie Hall*. The movie convinced him, Canby said, that "Woody Allen is America's Ingmar Bergman . . . It's about time that we recognized Woody Allen as one of our most original, most personal, most passionate, most introspective filmmakers . . . I haven't seen an American film in years that was as seriously interested in the relations between men and women as *Annie Hall*."

But Woody Allen, in spite of substantial critical and financial success, remains uncertain of the degree to which he has succeeded in rendering his original idea into the reality of film. "Me—I never like my movies. They're never anywhere near what I set out to make. Occasionally, individual moments come out well, but most of the movies are not as good as they were in my mind. I'm hoping right after *Annie Hall* is premiered, I'll never have to hear about it or see it again. Nothing would please me more.

"I don't have that big a following," he added. "I mean, I have a moderate following, not enormous, and they may be loyal, although I'm not too sure about that, and I suppose some of them, if they're there, identify with my particular problems, and others feel confident because they don't have those particular problems."

Woody Allen believes that his willingness to make films for his "moderate following" is one of the reasons for his success in movies. His guiding philosophy in dealing with United

Artists can be succinctly summed up: "Don't overreach."

"... I mean, I have a nice, simple gentlemen's agreement with the studio. The best of anyone, artistically. I've traded the idea of making millions and millions from them for my artistic control. For instance, I hate having my pictures shown on TV—everything sliced up with deodorant commercials—and they've agreed they won't allow that as long as my movies make a profit. Not necessarily a huge profit—none of mine ever have.

"UA doesn't get to approve scripts, my casting, anything. I just come to them with a movie which can be made for $2 million, at the very most $3 million, which is not a lot today. The movie will not be starring Barbra Streisand or Robert Redford—I have no real interest in working with stars—therefore it won't cost so much.

"No, I am *not* a star, in the sense that, say, Redford is. I'm just not that bankable, my pictures don't make what his do. I don't really even know who my audience is ... A picture of mine'll do great in Omaha, bomb in Des Moines. Why? It's beyond me.

"But nothing of mine's ever *lost* any money, so I can go on as I want, UA says, as long as I keep my costs down and we all make a little, they'll let me alone. No, I'm not hurting for money, but I couldn't retire. Maybe take one year off—no more—to write what I want to write next ..."

* * * * * *

Several months after *Annie Hall* was released, Woody Allen began the pre-production work for his next movie. All the years of hints of wanting to do a "serious" movie had come to fruition. He had done a "serious" comedy and it had been a huge success. Now he would do a serious film. Period.

chapter 8

A Break

With the Past

IN MARCH, 1965, WOODY ALLEN was 29, looked 17 and had just finished working on *What's New, Pussycat?*, a movie that, for all its abominations, was for Woody Allen the big breakthrough. Before *What's New, Pussycat?* he was a bright, young stand-up comedian who might well have divided his life between night clubs, Las Vegas and *The Tonight Show*.

At that time, his ambitions were modest. "All I want is not to be taken seriously," Woody said wistfully. "I have no great insight into poverty or integration or their relation to history, death or God. I just want to tell jokes."

In March, 1977, Woody Allen was 41, looked 29 and was awaiting the release of *Annie Hall*, his sixth movie as director and writer. And now he very much wanted to be taken seriously. Even before *Annie Hall* was in the theaters, he was working on a new screenplay, this one as serious, at least in intention, as anything ever written by that uniquely American, brooding theatrical genius, Eugene O'Neill.

"Maybe not quite on that level of profundity, but yes, on that level of ... functioning. Yeah, a real tragedy ... I haven't said any of this before, publicly—but it's all that interests me next, as a writer.

"No, I haven't pushed myself in that direction; if anything, I'm resisting it, it's pushing me. A quantum leap. I will go with it, and either I'll do it well, or make a fool of

171

myself . . . Of course, if what I write in this vein comes out very badly, it will just stay sitting in the drawer."

But of course he *had* said it before, many times. In 1972, to cite one example, Woody said, "This summer, for the first time in my life, I'm going to write a deadly serious play—a pure drama."

His old friend, Dick Cavett, however, thought it would never happen. "Woody will never let go of the comic character," Cavett said. "Of all the things he's worked on, the one that took the most energy and revision was his own stand-up routine. And he never turns off his comic mind. We can be talking away at a cash register after lunch and he'll start scribbling a new one-liner on the back of the check."

In recent years, however, Woody Allen has become increasingly dissatisfied, not just with his own work, but with the entire genre of comedy. "All my films have been personal failures. This is not to say that an audience, not knowing the grandiose plans I had in mind when I undertook the project, can't go in and find something to enjoy . . . But none of them leaves me with a good feeling. I finish them and I don't want to see them again. I can only see all the mistakes and embarrassing moments. I can't get to the point where they're a kick for me.

"I've always felt I was indictable as a film maker on the basis of triviality. That's my own biggest self-criticism and one that I accept unhesitatingly from anyone who wants to level it. I thought my films were funny, but finally funny in the way—and I don't mean qualitatively—that Chaplin two-reelers were funny. That real out-and-out comedy; slapstick and craziness and silliness. But I feel that's a dead end to work in, because, you know, if it's just a question of getting laughs for an hour and a half, I know now I can do that.

"It's a personal view, but I have a lesser opinion of comedy. It's much harder to do than serious film making—it's real hard to make an audience laugh and keep them laughing—but if it's tough, so what? In the long run, I get more enjoyment out of a film like *Persona* than *The General* or *City Lights*. A comedy, for me, has the quality of being a little dessert, a diversion. It's fun to see a Keaton or a Chaplin film—and, of course, I have an irresistible enjoyment of the

Marx Brothers; but to me it's all second features. The real meat and potatoes are serious films.

"The type of drama that interests me most is not indigenous to the United States—I'm not sure any American film maker makes the kind of movie I want to make. I don't want to do films like *Bonnie and Clyde* or *Mean Streets* or *Badlands* or *Nashville*—though I admire all of them. To me, American serious movies always have one foot in entertainment—and I like more personal drama, though there may not be a market for it. The drama I like is what you see in the plays of O'Neill and Strindberg and Ibsen—and in foreign films.

In other words, Woody Allen wants to make a movie that is "serious, dead serious. Not middle serious, not like Truffaut, not bittersweet, but very heavy stuff, *really* heavy . . . It's a terrible thing to say—almost masochistic in a way—but in (Ingmar Bergman's) *The Seventh Seal* that constant, unrelieved gloom, the intensity of feeling, the religious solemnity, are very pleasureable to me—it's hypnotic. That slow pacing—well, a movie like that just can't be paced slow enough for me.

"The questions and feelings in Bergman's films are what interest me—an investigation of spiritual values and faith. It would be very different for someone like myself—with my background and reputation—suddenly to come up with a serious, religious film . . . The line between the kind of solemnity I want and comedy is very, very thin. That's why it's so easy to satirize Bergman. If you bring drama off, you hit people at the most profound level, but tenth-rate Bergman or O'Neill is like soap opera. My biggest fear is that I'll write a mawkish and embarrassing soap opera and not know it.

"The fundamental thing behind *all* motivation and *all* activity is the constant struggle against annihilation and against death. It's absolutely stupefying in its terror, and it renders anyone's accomplishments meaningless. As Camus wrote, it's not only that he dies or that man dies, but that you struggle to do a work of art that will last and then realize that the universe itself is not going to exist after a period of time. Until those issues are resolved within each person—religiously or psychologically or existentially—the social and political issues will never be resolved, except in a slapdash way. They'll never be solved as long as people wake up each day and worry that they're finite, that they don't know why they're here or where they're going or when they're going to die."

Woody paused and then said very intensely: "People have to stop and think what their priorities are."

After what must have involved months of soul-searching and at least a modicum of trepidation, Woody Allen set his priorities and decided that he had to risk the big failure, the absurdity of the clown who yearns to play Hamlet. In the fall of 1977, Woody began directing his seventh film. As in the six that preceded it, he wrote the screenplay as well.

There are two radical departures from the past: the new movie is not a comedy and Woody will not appear in it, thus minimizing the risk of absurdity. The clown who wants to *direct* Hamlet and fails is less ridiculous than the clown who wants to *act* Hamlet and fails.

"You could characterize me as apprehensive, insecure and totally out of my element," Woody said shortly after filming began. "Right now, I'm interested in making myself as uncomfortable as possible, immersing myself, committing myself to an area of film making I know nothing about. This movie is not a comedy at all; it's a very serious, a totally experimental project for me. I'll be dealing with a large group of actors and actresses, trying to encourage them to bring scenes to life that are not funny, but complicated and serious.

"In a way, it's like taking a cold shower. But I feel so long as I am not in movies for the inane nonsense of creating hit films, I'm doing the right thing to take a chance. *Annie Hall* was a big success for me, but I don't want to make the mistake of repeating myself. It would be very easy for me to play into my strengths, to come up with another box-office hit. But I wanted to depart in some way; maybe I'm departing too radically, I don't know ... I just know that I have to do things I'm not sure I can do and I have to be prepared to fail with them. Even if this movie is a total disaster, I still will have grown. I will have learned more about myself, about my weaknesses, my limitations."

The new movie's cast includes some of the best actors now working: Geraldine Page, Maureen Stapleton, E.G. Marshall, Sam Waterston, Marybeth Hurt, Richard Jordan and, of course, Diane Keaton. "Diane has a role no bigger or smaller than any of the other leading actors in the movie," Woody said. "This is an ensemble piece, and I have a tremendous cast, so the only one who can mess things up is me."

Nor would Woody divulge any details about plot or story. "I'm secretive about it," he explained, "so that in case anything goes wrong, I can change the mistakes before anyone knows about them."

For years, Woody Allen has cut his terrors down to size by making jokes about them. Now, apparently, he is going to tackle at least a few of them head-on. The strategy may be futile, the results may be pretentious. It's also possible the strategy may prove brilliant and the resulting film turn out to be an illuminating and enduring piece of cinematic art.

Which is a far distance to travel for a scrawny, near-sighted kid who was forced to attend a school for emotionally disturbed teachers.

THE WORKS OF WOODY ALLEN

What's New, Pussycat? Screenplay by Woody Allen. Directed by Clive Donner. Produced by Charles K. Feldman. A June, 1965 United Artists release, starring Peter O'Toole, Peter Sellers, Romy Schneider, Paula Prentiss, Capucine and Woody Allen. Running time: 108 minutes.

What's Up, Tiger Lily? Soundtrack written by Woody Allen and produced by Henry G. Saperstein and Reuben Bercovitch for what was originally a Japanese movie in the style of the Hollywood hard-boiled detective genre. Released by American International Pictures in November, 1966.

Don't Drink the Water. A comedy in two acts and nine scenes by Woody Allen. Staged by Stanley Prager. Setting and lighting by Jo Mielziner. Presented by David Merrick in association with Jack Rollins and Charles Joffe. Starring Kay Medford, Lou Jacobi and Anita Gillette, the play opened at the Morosco Theatre in New York on November 17, 1966.

Take the Money and Run. Original screenplay by Woody Allen and Mickey Rose. Directed by Woody Allen. Produced by Charles H. Joffe. Released in August, 1969 by the Cinerama Releasing Corporation. Starring Woody Allen and Janet Margolin. Running time: 85 minutes.

Don't Drink the Water (movie version). Screenplay by R.S. Allen and Harvey Bullock based on the play by Woody Allen. Directed by Howard Morris. Produced by Charles H. Joffe. Presented by Joseph E. Levine and starring Jackie Gleason and Estelle Parsons. Released by Avco Embassy in November, 1969. Running time: 98 minutes.

Play It Again, Sam. A comedy by Woody Allen. Staged by Joseph Hardy. Setting by William Ritman; lighting by Martin Aronstein; costumes by Ann Roth. Presented by David Merrick, in association with Jack Rollins and Charles Joffe, the cast included Woody Allen, Diane Keaton, Tony Roberts and Jerry Lacy as Bogart. Opened at the Broadhurst Theatre in New York on February 12, 1969.

Bananas. Original screenplay by Woody Allen and Mickey Rose. Directed by Woody Allen. Produced by Jack Grossberg and released in April, 1971 by United Artists, the cast included Woody Allen, Louise Lasser, Carlos Montalban and Howard Cosell. Running time: 82 minutes.

Play It Again, Sam (movie version). Screenplay by Woody Allen, based on his Broadway play. Directed by Herbert Ross, produced by Arthur P. Jacobs and released by Paramount Pictures in May, 1972. There were few cast changes. Woody Allen, Diane Keaton and Tony Roberts also took featured roles in the movie. Once again, Jerry Lacy played Bogey. Running time: 87 minutes.

Everything You Always Wanted to Know about Sex but Were Afraid to Ask.
Screenplay by Woody Allen based on the book by Dr. David Reuben.
Directed by Woody Allen. Produced by Charles Joffe and released by United
Artists in August, 1972. The cast included John Carradine, Lou Jacobi,
Louise Lasser, Anthony Quayle, Tony Randall, Burt Reynolds and Woody
Allen. Running time: 87 minutes.

Getting Even.   By Woody Allen. A collection of comic essays most of
which originally appeared in *The New Yorker.* Random House, 1972.

Sleeper.   Original screenplay by Woody Allen and Marshall Brickman.
Directed by Woody Allen. Produced by Jack Grossberg. Executive producer,
Charles Joffe. Released by United Artists in December, 1973. The cast in-
cluded Woody Allen and Diane Keaton. Running time: 88 minutes.

Without Feathers.   By Woody Allen. A collection of comic essays. Random
House, 1975.

Love and Death.   Written and directed by Woody Allen. Produced by Charles
Joffe. Released by United Artists in June, 1975. Starring Woody Allen and
Diane Keaton. Running time: 89 minutes.

The Front.   Screenplay by Walter Bernstein. Directed by Martin Ritt.
Released by Columbia Pictures in September, 1976. Starring Woody Allen
and Zero Mostel.

Annie Hall.   Screenplay by Woody Allen and Marshall Brickman. Directed
by Woody Allen. Produced by Charles H. Joffe. Released by United Artists
in April, 1977. The cast includes Woody Allen, Diane Keaton, Tony Roberts,
Colleen Dewhurst, Carol Kane and Paul Simon. *Annie Hall* won the N.Y.
Critics Circle Award for Best Movie of 1977.

index